P9-DYE-166

PENGUIN BOOKS

THE TE OF PIGLET

Benjamin Hoff is an Oregon writer, photographer, musician, and composer with a fondness for Forests and Bears. And Piglets. A Bachelor of Arts (he thinks his degree was in Asian Art, but then, he hasn't looked at it for a while, and it may not be), he was until recently a Japanese-trained fine pruning specialist. He now writes full time. Well, most of the time. The rest of the time he practices Taoist yoga, T'ai Chi Ch'uan, stunt kite-flying, boomerang shaping and (ouch!) throwing, and Taoist tennis, whatever that is. He also enjoys sleeping and lying about on the floor.

He is the author of *The Tao of Pooh*, *The Te of Piglet*, and *The Singing Creek Where the Willows Grow: The Rediscovered Diary of Opal Whiteley*.

Benjamin Hoff

THE TE OF PIGLET

PENGUIN BOOKS

PENGUIN BOOKS
Published by the Penguin Group
Penguin Books USA Inc., 375 Hudson Street,
New York, New York 10014, U.S.A.
Penguin Books Ltd, 27 Wrights Lane, London W8 5TZ, England
Penguin Books Australia Ltd, Ringwood, Victoria, Australia
Penguin Books Canada Ltd, 10 Alcorn Avenue,
Toronto, Ontario, Canada M4V 3B2
Penguin Books (N.Z.) Ltd, 182–190 Wairau Road,
Auckland 10, New Zealand

Penguin Books Ltd, Registered Offices:
Harmondsworth, Middlesex, England

First published in the United States of America by Dutton,
an imprint of New American Library,
a division of Penguin Books USA Inc., 1992
Published in Penguin Books 1993

10 9 8 7 6 5 4 3 2 1

THE LIBRARY OF CONGRESS HAS CATALOGUED THE HARDCOVER AS FOLLOWS:
Hoff, Benjamin, 1946–
The te of Piglet/Benjamin Hoff.
p. cm.
Summary: The author and the characters from the Pooh books engage in dialogue elucidating the Taoist principle of Te, the Way of the Small.
ISBN 0-525-93496-0 (hc.)
ISBN 0 14 02.3016 5 (pbk.)
1. Milne, A. A. (Alan Alexander), 1882–1956—Characters—Piglet.
2. Milne, A. A. (Alan Alexander), 1882–1956—Religion.   3. Size perception in literature.   4. Piglet (Fictitious character).   5. Taoism in literature.
6. Taoism.   [1. Milne, A. A.(Alan Alexander), 1882–1956—Characters.
2. Taoism.]   I. Title.
PR6025.I65Z69   1992
823´.912—dc20   92–4503

Printed in the United States of America
Set in Perpetua and Caledonia

For Lan Ts'ai-ho

"It is hard to be brave," said Piglet, sniffing slightly, "when you're only a Very Small Animal."

Rabbit, who had begun to write very busily, looked up and said:

"It is because you are a very small animal that you will be Useful in the adventure before us."

CONTENTS

THE TE OF PIGLET

WHAT?
ANOTHER ONE?

One day not long ago, I found Piglet sitting by himself on the writing table, gazing wistfully out the window. I asked what he was doing . . .

"Oh, just wishing," he replied.

"Wishing what?" I asked.

"Nothing, really," he said, turning pinker than usual around the ears.

"You know I won't make fun of you if you tell me."

"Well . . . I was only wishing—"

"Yes?"

"Only wishing . . . That someday someone would notice me."

"*I* notice you."

"I only meant—that is, most everyone notices *Pooh* . . ."

"Yes, most everyone does. Ever since the Pooh books came out, years ago."

"And now, especially," said Piglet. "Because of you-know-what."

"Ah, yes," I said. "Just for a moment, I'd forgotten."

And then it was my turn to gaze wistfully out the window, remembering the spring of 1982. For it was then that Dutton released a book of mine called *The Tao of Pooh*. It seemed so long ago, somehow . . .

The Tao of Pooh began as a reaction to what I considered an unfortunate situation. English-language writings on the Chinese philosophy of Taoism—which, I had come to realize, was far more than "Chinese," and far more than "philoso-phy"—had for many years been dominated by scholarly sorts who seemed more interested in cat-aloguing and bickering over Minute Particulars than in communicating the practical wisdom of Taoist principles.

For most of my life I had been learning those principles from various Taoist teachers—some of-ficial and some not, some Chinese and some not, some in human form and (the best instructors of them all) some not. I saw them being muddled and mutilated in the "Taoist" writings of scholars who were not Taoists, who had not been taught by Taoists, and who did not practice Taoist skills and exercises—yet who monopolized the subject of Taoism and sneered at anyone who suggested that there was more to it than what they told.

I would come across such things as a description by the Taoist writer Chuang-tse of some tactics of swordsmanship, translated into nonsense by an Authority apparently ignorant of even the basic precepts of Taoist martial arts . . . And I would ask myself if there weren't something that could be done about that sort of thing.

Then one day, while quoting to someone from A. A. Milne's *Winnie-the-Pooh*, I got an Idea. I could write a book explaining Taoism through the characters in *Winnie-the-Pooh* and *The House at Pooh Corner*. That would, it seemed to me, release Taoist wisdom from the grip of the Overacademics and restore to it the childlike awareness and sense of humor that they had taken away.

On being told of the Idea, certain Eeyores advised me against attempting anything of the sort. But following the advice of Eeyores has rarely seemed A Particularly Good Thing for Me to Do.

Quite the contrary: If the Eeyores are against something, I tend to think there might be something to it.

And so I wrote the manuscript, it was published, and that (I thought) was the end of the matter. But it wasn't. It was more or less the beginning.

Before *The Tao of Pooh*, one would not have heard many nonscholarly or nonmystical Westerners discussing Taoism. But today Taoist principles are described in publications on business, science, psychology, health, sports, music, art, writing, computer programming, and other subjects. They are discussed in corporate-strategy sessions, high school and college classes, and other gatherings of various kinds. And (according to what I've read and heard) the book most often recommended to explain Taoist principles is *The Tao of Pooh*. Colleges use the book as a text on Taoism, psychiatrists give copies to their patients, ministers quote from it in their sermons, Chinese martial arts instructors read it to their students, and so on. I have even been told that some motel owners put it in their rental units. It would seem that *The Tao of Pooh* (also known as *Le Tao de Pooh*, *Tao enligt Puh*, *Nalle Puh ja Tao*, and such) is known and liked around the world. And that, I must say, has pleased Pooh enormously.

"Oh, Pooh!" said everybody else except Eeyore.

"Thank-you," growled Pooh.

But Eeyore was saying to himself, "This writing business. Pencils and what-not. Over-rated, if you ask me. Silly stuff. Nothing in it."

And so *The Tao of Pooh* has become known as a Remarkable Success. And until fairly recently, I'd considered that The End. I'd explained Taoist principles. I'd entertained with Pooh and friends. There were other things I wanted to do, other things I wanted to be associated with. "Stop this Remarkable Success, please," I asked. "I'd like to get off." But no one wanted to let me off. "No, I don't intend a *Tao of Pooh* sequel. I don't like sequels. Thank you very much. Good-bye."

But slowly and softly—so softly that for a long time I was unaware of it—something began to steal into my consciousness. A small voice was trying to catch my attention. After a while, I realized that it was Piglet's. Finally I sat down and listened.

And after listening for a while, I began to take notes . . . There was more to be said, Piglet pointed out—but no one was saying it, and it was needed today. It would be needed even more, he said, in the years to come. Another book needn't be a "sequel"; it could be a companion book, as *The House at Pooh Corner* is to *Winnie-the-Pooh*. Why did I listen to Piglet? The answer lies in the past.

In my childhood, when the *Pooh* stories were first read to me, I immediately developed a fondness for Piglet—from the beginning, he was my favorite of the *Pooh* characters. That I knew, but I didn't know why. By now I know why. And I hope that before you have finished reading this book, you will know why, too.

INTERJECTION

We had wanted to make this the Introduction, but something else managed to put itself ahead of it. So we decided that we couldn't call this an Introduction, after all.

We asked Owl, who's the one to consult in matters of this sort, what one calls an Introduction that comes after something else. "An Interjection," he knowingly replied. And since Owl says that this is an Interjection, that is what it is.

Now, the first thing—

"Am *I* in it?" asked Pooh.

"Oh—Pooh. I didn't know you were here."

"Hardly anyone ever seems to notice," said Pooh sadly.

"Of course you're in it, Pooh. Now."

"That's good," he said, cheering up considerably.

What we want to explain in this Interjection—

"This *what*?" asked Pooh.
"Interjection. What we're doing now."
"Oh. Is that anything like an Interruption?"
"Well, something of the sort. I imagine."

Anyway, what we'd like to do in this Interruption is to explain that—we'll have to say this softly—this book isn't just about Pooh.

"Beg pardon?" said Pooh. "Did someone say something?"
"I didn't hear anything," said I.
"Oh," said Pooh.
"Er, Pooh—isn't that a rare bird in the tree outside the window? Or is it a fish?"
"I don't see anything in the tree," said Pooh.
"I'm sure it's a fish. One of the rare ones."
"It must be," said Pooh. "If it's up a tree."
"Do go and find out, won't you, Pooh? Here, I'll open the door for you. Take a good look. Goodbye."

* * *

Yes, this is not so much a *Pooh* book as it is a *Piglet* book. In these pages, it will be the timid, yearning Piglet, rather than the comfortable, contented Pooh, who shows us the Way. In other words, we'll be looking at things from a slightly different angle. Since we are dealing with a more timid animal this time, this book may seem a bit more serious than its predecessor. But—

"Ah—there you are," said Rabbit. "Piglet's fallen into the wastebasket."

Perhaps *serious* isn't quite the word we want. Perhaps—

"*Help! Help!*"

—a better word would be *quieter*.

CRASH!!!***?
"What in heaven's name was that?"
"Tigger's rescued him," said Rabbit.
"Poor Piglet. Tell him I'll be there immediately."

Excuse me.

THE—WHAT WAS THAT
AGAIN?—OF PIGLET

One day when the sun had come back over the Forest, bringing with it the scent of May, and all the streams of the Forest were tinkling happily to find themselves their own pretty shape again, and the little pools lay dreaming of the life they had seen and the big things they had done, and in the warmth and quiet of the Forest the cuckoo was trying over his voice carefully and listening to see if he liked it, and wood-pigeons were complaining gently to themselves in their lazy comfortable way that it was the other fellow's fault, but it didn't matter very much; on such a day as this Christopher Robin whistled in a special way he had, and Owl came flying out of the Hundred Acre Wood to see what was wanted.

"Ah—Pooh and Piglet. Come in and make yourselves comfortable. You're just in time."

"In time for what?" asked Pooh hopefully. "For a bit of—"

"For a bit of Taoism."

"Oh."

"Is it dangerous?" asked Piglet.

"Certainly not. You know what Taoism is."

"Yes," said Piglet, not quite sure. "Of course."

"You see, before we go any further, we need to explain Taoism."

"Didn't we do that already?" asked Pooh.

"That was in *The Tao of Pooh*. We need to say something Explanatory here, as well. Just in case."

"In case of what?" asked Piglet nervously.

"In case . . . Well, just in case. I suppose we could have Pooh say something about it, but he probably can't remember what it is."

"Of course I can," replied Pooh. "It's . . . That is, it's something like . . . Or is it? What I mean is . . ."

"That's what I thought."

"When you explained Taoism before," said Piglet, "you and Pooh went to China. If we do that, I'll need to pack some things."

"No, we won't be going to China. We're going to stay right here."

"That's good," said Pooh, wandering over to the kitchen.

"Because we'll begin with a Taoist explanation of the Origin of Taoism. And we might as well stay where we are, because wherever in the world we may be at any moment is where Taoism started— whether or not it was known there by that name. It began before the time of the Great Separation . . ."

Thousands of years ago, man lived in harmony with the rest of the natural world. Through what we would today call Telepathy, he communicated with animals, plants, and other forms of life—none of which he considered "beneath" himself, only different, with different jobs to perform. He worked side by side with earth angels and nature spirits, with whom he shared responsibility for taking care of the world.

The earth's atmosphere was very different from what it is now, with a great deal more vegetation-supporting moisture. A tremendous variety of vegetable, fruit, seed, and grain food was available. Because of such a diet, and a lack of unnatural strain, human life span was many times longer than what it is today. The killing of animals for food or "sport" was unthinkable. Man lived at peace with himself and the various life forms, whom he considered his teachers and friends.

But gradually at first, and then with increasing intensity, man's Ego began to grow and assert itself. Finally, after it had caused many unpleasant incidents, the consensus was reached that man should go out into the world alone, to learn a necessary lesson. The connections were broken.

On his own, feeling alienated from the world he had been created from, cut off from the full extent of its abundance, man was no longer happy. He began to search for the happiness he had lost. When he found something that reminded him of it, he tried to possess it and accumulate more— thereby introducing Stress into his life. But searching for lasting happiness and accumulating temporary substitutes for it brought him no satisfaction.

As he was no longer able to hear what the other forms of life were saying, he could only try to understand them through their actions, which he often misinterpreted. Because he was no longer cooperating with the earth angels and nature spirits for the good of all, but was attempting to manipulate the earth forces for his benefit alone, plants began to shrivel and die. With less vegetation to draw up and give off moisture, the planet's atmosphere became drier, and deserts appeared. A relatively small number of plant species survived, which grew smaller and tougher with passing time. Eventually they lost the radiant colors and abundant fruit of their ancestors. Man's life span began to shorten accordingly, and diseases appeared and spread. Because of the decreasing variety of food available to him—and his growing insensitivity—man began to kill and eat his friends the animals. They soon learned to flee from his approach and became increasingly shy and suspicious of human motives and behavior. And so the separation grew. After several generations, few people had any idea of what life had once been like.

As man became more and more manipulative of and violent toward the earth, and as his social and spiritual world narrowed to that of the human race alone, he became more and more manipulative of and violent toward his own kind. Men began to kill and enslave each other, creating armies and empires, forcing those who looked, talked, thought, and acted differently from them to submit to what they thought was best.

Life became so miserable for the human race

that, around two to three thousand years ago, perfected spirits began to be born on earth in human
form, to teach the truths that had largely been
forgotten. But by then humanity had grown so divided, and so insensitive to the universal laws operating in the natural world, that those truths were
only partially understood.

As time passed, the teachings of the perfected
spirits were changed, for what one might call political reasons, by the all-too-human organizations
that inherited them. Those who came into prominence within the organizations wanted power over
others. They downplayed the importance of non-
human life forms and eliminated from the teachings statements claiming that those forms had
souls, wisdom, and divine presence—and that the
heaven they were in touch with was a state of
Unity with the Divine that could be attained by
anyone who put aside his ego and followed the
universal laws. The power-hungry wanted their followers to believe that heaven was a place to which
some people—and only people—went after death,
a place that could be reached by those who had
the approval of *their* organizations. So not even
the perfected spirits were able to restore the
wholeness of truth, because of interference by the
human ego.

Down through the centuries, accounts of the
Great Separation, and of the Golden Age that existed before it, have been passed on by the sensitive and wise. Today in the industrial West, they
are classified as mere legends and myths—fantasies
believed in by the credulous and unsophisticated,
stories based only on imagination and emotion.
Despite the fact that quite a few people have seen
and communicated with earth angels and nature
spirits, and that more than one spiritual community has grown luscious fruits and vegetables by
cooperating with them and following their instruc-
tions, descriptions of these beings are generally
dismissed as "fairy tales." And, although colored
and simplified accounts of the Great Separation can
be found in the holy books of the world's religions,
it is doubtful that many followers of those religions
strongly believe in them.

However, a number of pre-Separation skills,
beliefs, and practices have been preserved. On the
North American continent, they are passed on in
some of what remains of native teachings—those
of the "Indians." In Europe they have largely died
out, but traces of their influence can still be seen
in such comparatively recent phenomena as stone
circles and the marking of "ley lines" (called
"dragon veins" by the Chinese)—channels along

which earth energy is concentrated. In Tibet, until
the Communist invasion, ancient ways were preserved in Tibetan Buddhism, many of the secrets
and practices of which predate Buddhism by thousands of years. In Japan, they can be found in some
of the rituals and beliefs of the Shinto ("spirit way")
folk religion. In China, they have been passed on
through Taoism. And, despite violent opposition
from China's Communist government, they continue to be passed on today.

Briefly, Taoism is a way of living in harmony
with *Tao*, the Way of the Universe, the character
of which is revealed in the workings of the natural
world. Taoism could be called either a philosophy
or a religion, or neither, since in its various forms
it does not match up with Western ideas or defini-
tions of either one.

In China, Taoism is what might be called the
counterbalance of Confucianism, the codified, ritu-
alized teachings of K'ung Fu-tse, or "Master K'ung,"
better known in the West as Confucius. Although
Confucianism is not a religion in the Western
sense, it could be said to bear a certain resemblance to puritanical Christianity in its man-cen-
tered, nature-ignoring outlook, its emphasis on
rigid conformity, and its authoritarian, No-Non-

sense attitude toward life. Confucianism concerns itself mostly with human relations—with social and political rules and hierarchies. Its major contributions have been in the areas of government, business, clan and family relations, and ancestor reverence. Its most vital principles are Righteousness, Propriety, Benevolence, Loyalty, Good Faith, Duty, and Justice. Briefly stated, Confucianism deals with the individual's place within the group.

In contrast, Taoism deals primarily with the individual's relationship to the world. Taoism's contributions have been mostly scientific, artistic, and spiritual. From Taoism came Chinese science, medicine, gardening, landscape painting, and nature poetry. Its key principles are Natural Simplicity, Effortless Action, Spontaneity, and Compassion. The most easily noticed difference between Confucianism and Taoism is emotional, a difference in *feeling*: Confucianism is stern, regimented, patriarchal, often severe; Taoism is happy, gentle, child-like, and serene—like its favorite symbol, that of flowing water.

Taoism is classically viewed as the teachings of three men: Lao-tse ("Master Lao"), author of the major Taoist classic, the *Tao Te Ching*, which is said to have been written around twenty-five hundred years ago; Chuang-tse ("Master Chuang"), author of several works and founder of a school of writers and philosophers during the Warring States period, approximately two thousand years ago; and the semilegendary Yellow Emperor, who ruled over forty-five hundred years ago, and to whom are attributed various meditative, alchemical, and medicinal principles and practices. These three were the great organizers and communicators of Taoist thought, rather than its founders; for, as we have said, what is now known as Taoism began before any of them were born, in what Chuang-tse called the Age of Perfect Virtue:

> In the Age of Perfect Virtue, men lived among the animals and birds as members of one large family. There were no distinctions between "superior" and "inferior" to separate one man or species from another. All retained their natural Virtue and lived in the state of pure simplicity. . . .
>
> In the Age of Perfect Virtue, wisdom and ability were not singled out as extraordinary. The wise were seen merely as higher branches on humanity's tree, growing a little closer to the sun. People behaved correctly, without knowing that to be

Righteousness and Propriety. They loved and respected each other, without calling that Benevolence. They were faithful and honest, without
considering that to be Loyalty. They kept their
word, without thinking of Good Faith. In their
everyday conduct, they helped and employed
each other, without considering Duty. They did
not concern themselves with Justice, as there was
no *in*justice. Living in harmony with themselves,
each other, and the world, their actions left no trace,
and so we have no physical record of their existence.*

Ever since the Great Separation, Taoists have
concerned themselves with attaining the state of
Perfect Virtue, through discarding whatever pre-
vents harmony with Tao.

And with that mention of Virtue, we come to
an explanation of the title of this book.

"I wondered when you were going to get
around to that," said Piglet.

"So did I. But, anyway . . ."

First of all, we'd better explain that the Chinese character *Te*, as in "The *Te* of Piglet," is pro-

*This and other selections from classical oriental texts are my
own translations and adaptations.—B.H.

nounced *DEH*, more or less. If you want to be
particular, you can put a bit of an "r" sound at the
end: *DEHr*. If you want to be even more particular, you can pronounce it halfway between *DEHr*
and *DUHr*. And—

"And if you want to be more particular than
that," interrupted Eeyore, "you can take a corre-
spondence course."

"Oh—Eeyore. I didn't know you were here.
I thought you were out in your swamp."

"Since we're being particular about things,"
said Eeyore, "it's a *bog*—B-O-G. Yes, I was there.
Then I made the mistake of coming here. And
now, having heard all I care to of this, I shall
return."

"Well, don't let us detain you."

"So much for *explanations*," muttered Eeyore,
on his way out the door.

"Eeyore's that way, isn't he?" said Piglet.

"Not all the time," I said. "Occasionally he's
worse."

As we were saying, *Te* is pronounced *DEH*.
In classical Chinese, it is written two ways. The
first joins the character for "upright" to the charac-

ter for "heart." Its meaning is *virtue*. The second way adds the character for "left foot," which in Chinese signifies "stepping out." Its meaning is *virtue in action*.

Te is not, as its English-language equivalent suggests, a one-size-fits-all sort of goodness or admired behavior that can be recognized as essentially the same no matter who possesses it. It is instead a quality of special character, spiritual strength, or hidden potential unique to the individual—something that comes from the Inner Nature of things. And something, we might add, that the individual who possesses it may be quite unaware of—as is the case with Piglet through most of the *Pooh* stories.

In this book, we are concerned with the transformation of Virtue into Virtue That Steps Out. And Piglet, we believe, is the *Pooh* animal best suited to demonstrate the process—because in the *Pooh* stories it is Piglet, and only Piglet, who undergoes just such a transformation.

VERY SMALL ANIMAL

The Piglet lived in a very grand house in the middle of a beech-tree, and the beech-tree was in the middle of the forest, and the Piglet lived in the middle of the house. Next to his house was a piece of broken board which had: "TRESPASSERS W" on it. When Christopher Robin asked the Piglet what it meant, he said it was his grandfather's name, and had been in the family for a long time. Christopher Robin said you *couldn't* be called Trespassers W, and Piglet said yes, you could, because his grandfather was, and it was short for Trespassers Will, which was short of Trespassers William. And his grandfather had had two names in case he lost one—Trespassers after an uncle, and William after Trespassers.

And so we are introduced to Piglet, in the third chapter of *Winnie-the-Pooh*: Piglet, who

craves security (he lives in the middle of a house
in the middle of a tree in the middle of a forest);
Piglet, who wants to be Somebody (so he invents
a grandfather named Trespassers William); Piglet,
a squeaky voice with pink cheeks; Piglet, the Very
Small Animal. Unlike Pooh, who simply Is and
Does, Piglet *Agonizes*.

For example, when Piglet and Pooh fell into
the Gravel Pit . . .

"Pooh," he went on nervously, and came a little
closer, "do you think we're in a Trap?"

Pooh hadn't thought about it at all, but now he
nodded. For suddenly he remembered how he
and Piglet had once made a Pooh Trap for Heffalumps, and he guessed what had happened. He
and Piglet had fallen into a Heffalump Trap for
Poohs! That was what it was.

"What happens when the Heffalump comes?"
asked Piglet tremblingly, when he had heard the
news.

"Perhaps he won't notice *you*, Piglet," said Pooh
encouragingly, "because you're a Very Small
Animal."

"But he'll notice *you*, Pooh."

"He'll notice *me*, and I shall notice *him*," said Pooh, thinking it out. "We'll notice each other for a long time, and then he'll say: 'Ho-*ho*!' "

Piglet shivered a little at the thought of that "Ho-*ho*!" and his ears began to twitch.

"W-what will *you* say?" he asked.

Pooh tried to think of something he would say, but the more he thought, the more he felt that there *is* no real answer to "Ho-*ho*!" said by a Heffalump in the sort of voice this Heffalump was going to say it in.

"I shan't say anything," said Pooh at last. "I shall just hum to myself, as if I was waiting for something."

"Then perhaps he'll say, 'Ho-*ho*!' again?" suggested Piglet anxiously.

"He will," said Pooh.

Piglet's ears twitched so quickly that he had to lean them against the side of the Trap to keep them quiet.

"He will say it again," said Pooh, "and I shall go on humming. And that will Upset him. Because when you say 'Ho-*ho*!' twice, in a gloating sort of way, and the other person only hums, you suddenly find, just as you begin to say it the third time—that—that—well, you find——"

What Pooh means to say is, it then isn't Ho-*ho*-ish anymore. At least, that's what we *think* he means.

"But he'll say something else," said Piglet.

"That's just it. He'll say: 'What's all this?' And then *I* shall say—and this is a very good idea, Piglet, which I've just thought of—*I* shall say: 'It's a trap for a Heffalump which I've made, and I'm waiting for the Heffalump to fall in.' And I shall go on humming. That will Unsettle him."

"Pooh!" cried Piglet. . . . "You've saved us!"

"Have I?" said Pooh, not feeling quite sure.

But Piglet was quite sure; and his mind ran on, and he saw Pooh and the Heffalump talking to each other, and he thought suddenly, and a little sadly, that it *would* have been rather nice if it had been Piglet and the Heffalump talking so grandly to each other, and not Pooh, much as he loved Pooh; because he really had more brain than Pooh, and the conversation would go better if he and not Pooh were doing one side of it, and it would be comforting afterwards in the evenings to look back on the day when he answered a Heffalump back as bravely as if the Heffalump wasn't there. It seemed so easy now. He knew just what he would say. . . .

And that's how it was in the Gravel Pit—until Christopher Robin came along, looked down, and saw Piglet and Pooh. Then things became a bit Complicated:

"Ho-*ho*!" said Christopher Robin loudly and suddenly.

Piglet jumped six inches in the air with Surprise and Anxiety, but Pooh went on dreaming.

"It's the Heffalump!" thought Piglet nervously. "Now, then!" He hummed in his throat a little, so that none of the words should stick, and then, in

the most delightfully easy way, he said: "Tra-la-la,
tra-la-la. . . ." But he didn't look round, because
if you look round and see a Very Fierce Heffalump
looking down at you, sometimes you forget what
you were going to say.

"Rum-tum-tum-tiddle-um," said Christopher Robin
in a voice like Pooh's. . . .

"He's said the wrong thing," thought Piglet anxiously. "He ought to have said, 'Ho-*ho*!' again.
Perhaps I had better say it for him." And, as
fiercely as he could, Piglet said, "Ho-*ho*!"

"How *did* you get there, Piglet?" said Christopher
Robin in his ordinary voice.

"This is Terrible," thought Piglet. "First he talks in Pooh's voice, and then he talks in Christopher Robin's voice, and he's doing it so as to Unsettle me." And being now Completely Unsettled, he said very quickly and squeakily: "This is a trap for Poohs, and I'm waiting to fall in it, ho-*ho*, what's all this, and then I say ho-*ho* again."

"*What?*" said Christopher Robin.

"A trap for ho-ho's," said Piglet huskily. "I've just made it, and I'm waiting for the ho-ho to come-come."

Not very impressive, we're afraid.

"Oh. Hello, Piglet. Who's that rough-looking man I've seen following you about lately?"

"He's my new Bodyguard," squeaked Piglet.

"*Bodyguard?* Why in the world do you need a *bodyguard?* Can't you look out for yourself?"

"I suppose so," replied Piglet. "But I feel so much more Secure this way."

"He looks pretty tough. I hope you checked his references."

"References?"

"Yes. From places he's worked before. Does

he have a bad record—arrests, jail sentences, that
sort of thing?"

"I—I don't *think* so," said Piglet.

"Well, I suppose it's all right. If you really
think you need protection. By the way—what's
happened to the old family silverware?"

"What?"

"You know—the silver knives, forks, spoons,
and things. They're not in the drawer where they
used to be. I just wondered if anything—"

"No," Piglet blurted out. "He couldn't have—
I mean, they *couldn't* be. They've been misplaced
or something. Yes, that's it. They *must* be. They
. . . I . . . Excuse me, I must be going. Good-
bye."

That's odd.

We might point out here that Taoism has always been fond of Very Small Animals. Aside from
animals themselves—which Confucianists saw as
mere things to eat, sacrifice, or pull plows and
wagons—the Very Small Animals of traditional,
Confucianist-dominated Chinese society were
women, children, and the poor. Stepped on by
greedy merchants, landholders, and government

officials, the poor were at the very bottom of the Confucianist social scale. To put it another way, they weren't on it at all. Women, even those of wealthy families—*especially* those of wealthy families—weren't much better off, as the Confucianists practiced arranged marriage, polygamy, foot-binding (foot-*breaking*, actually), and other customs so repressive to women that no one in today's West could comprehend them. Children didn't have a very jolly time of it, either. To the staunch Confucianist, children existed to carry on the family line, unquestioningly obey their parents in every matter, and take every care of them in their old age— not to have ideas, ideals, and interests of their own. Under Confucianism, a father could justifiably kill a son who disobeyed or disgraced him, as such behavior was considered criminal.

In contrast, Taoism held that respect was something one earned, and that if Big Daddy misbehaved, his family had the right to rebel. That applied to the emperor and his "family"—his subjects—as well: If the emperor was a tyrant, the people had the right to take him off the throne. High Confucianist officials lived in constant fear of Taoist- and Buddhist-influenced secret societies that were ever ready to defend the stepped-on and attempt to topple the Dragon Throne if conditions became intolerable, which they often did.

Taoist sympathies were always with the Underdog—with the outcasts and unfortunates of Chinese society, including those financially ruined by the tricks of corrupt merchants and officials and forced to become "Brothers of the Green Woods" (outlaws) and "Guests of Rivers and Lakes" (vagabonds). The Chinese martial arts were developed primarily by Taoists and Buddhist monks, in order to defend the defenseless and enable them to defend themselves. They might better be termed the *anti*-martial arts, as they were employed not only against armed bandits, but also against the soldiers of warlords and governing bodies, whenever they turned their swords against the weak. While Buddhist martial artists tended to concentrate on the "hard" forms of defense (from which evolved the forceful and direct *Karate* and *Tae Kwon Do*), Taoists tended to concentrate on the "soft" forms, such as the fluid and indirect *T'ai Chi Ch'üan* and *Pa Kua Chang* (similar to, but more sophisticated than, *Judo* and *Aikido*).

In countering what they saw as abuse of power, Taoist writers did with their communicative skills what Taoist martial artists did with disarming moves and pressure points. Utilizing the vehicles of literary fact and fiction, they publicized the misdeeds of the powerful and ridiculed the devious, the arrogant, the pompous, and the cruel. Although annoyed Confucianists often attempted to put an end to these writings, they were generally unsuccessful, as the sympathies of the common people were against them.

Considering that High and Mighty Confucianists tended to have little respect for animals, and that they sometimes referred to the "lesser" peoples of China as "pigs" and "dogs," it is not surprising that Taoist writers recorded many animal stories—descriptions of actual occurrences as well as imaginary tales—in which maligned creatures such as mice, snakes, and birds of prey demonstrate virtuous conduct that Prestigious People would do well to emulate. In these stories, the courage, affection, faithfulness, and honesty of animals are contrasted with the pretentiousness and hypocrisy of wealthy landholders, merchants, and government officials. As an early example, Chuang-tse wrote:

The Officer of Prayer went to the pigpen in his official robes, and spoke to the pigs. "Why should you complain?" he asked. "I will feed you grain for three months. Then I will fast for ten days—while you eat—and keep watch over you for three days after that. Then I will spread fresh mats and place you on the carved sacrificial stand, before dispatching you to the spirit world. Considering all that I will be doing for you, why should you feel uneasy?"

If the official had been truly concerned with the welfare of the pigs, he would have fed them bran and chaff and left them alone. But he looked at the situation from the point of view of his own prestige. He preferred to enjoy the robes and cap of his privileged office, and to ride about in an ornamented carriage—knowing that when *he* died, he would be carried in splendor to his grave, a magnificent canopy spread above his coffin. If he had been concerned with the welfare of the pigs, he would not have considered these things to be important.

Wealthy Confucianists weren't the only targets of Taoist writers. Like the Marx Brothers or Stan Laurel and Oliver Hardy, the Taoists satirized Big Ego at any level of society. This tendency can be seen in the following story, "The Pear Seed," by the Ch'ing Dynasty writer P'u Sung-ling:

A well-dressed farmer was selling his pears in the town marketplace. As they were large and delicious, he was soon taking in quite a bit of money. A passing Taoist, dressed in patched cotton and carrying a small shovel on his back, stopped by the farmer's wagon and asked for a pear. The farmer told him to go away. The Taoist refused to leave. The farmer grew angrier and angrier. Soon he was shouting at the top of his voice.

"But there are hundreds of pears in your wagon," the Taoist calmly pointed out. "I'm only asking for one. Why be so upset?"

More and more people gathered, attracted by the commotion. Some onlookers told the farmer to toss the poor man a bruised pear. The farmer refused. Finally, seeing that the uproar was about to turn into a riot, someone bought a pear and handed it to the Taoist. After warmly thanking his benefactor, the Taoist turned to the crowd.

"We followers of the Way are revolted by petty greed," he told them. "Let me share this beautiful fruit with you kind people."

No one wanted to take a piece of the Taoist's pear. The spectators insisted that he eat it himself.

"All I need is a seed to plant," the Taoist replied, "and then I'll be able to repay you." He ate the fruit, except for one small seed. With his little shovel he dug a hole, dropped the seed into it, and covered it over. Then he called for heated water. Someone brought some from a nearby shop. The crowd watched in intense fascination as the Taoist watered the ground where the seed was planted.

Suddenly a small shoot appeared, which quickly grew into a tree. Branches and leaves shot out in great profusion. The tree blossomed, then bore a tremendous crop of large, luscious pears.

The Taoist distributed the fruit among the spectators. Soon all of it was gone. Then, with his small shovel, he chopped down the tree. Waving to the crowd, he happily departed, dragging the tree behind him.

All this time, the greedy farmer had been staring, openmouthed. Now he turned back to his pears—only to find that they were gone. Shaking off the effects of the Taoist's spell, he realized what had happened to them. He saw that a section of his wagon's harnessing pole—the same diameter as the trunk of the "pear tree"—had been chopped away.

After a frantic search, the farmer found the pole leaning against a wall, where the Taoist had left it. As for the Taoist, he was nowhere to be seen. The crowd roared with laughter in appreciation of the instructive joke.

Did someone just come in? Oh.

"So you're Piglet's new bodyguard. Well, well."

"You got a *problem* with that, buddy?"

"No, not at all."

"Good. I wouldn't get any *ideas* if I was you, fella."

"Oh, yes you would. You'd get all sorts of ideas. Such as how easy it is to pull someone off his feet with a loose rug—like the one you're standing on."

"What're you *talkin'* about?"

"Oh, nothing. Just make yourself at home."

"T'anks."

In order to understand Taoist support of the Underdog, one needs to understand the Taoist attitude toward power, from the Power of the Universe on down. As with other matters, the Taoist view was historically more or less the opposite of the Confucianist.

The Confucianist conception of Heavenly Power, vague though it tended to be, bore a certain resemblance to the Middle Eastern, Old Testament image of God. The Confucianists called it *T'ien*—"Sky," "Heaven," or "Supreme Ruler." T'ien was seen as masculine, sometimes ferociously so. It needed to be appeased with sacrifices and rituals. It took sides; it granted authority. It transmitted sovereignty directly to the emperor, the Son of Heaven. From him, dominion spread downward and outward—from the highest officials to the lowest, from the major clans to the minor families. T'ien was imagined as dazzling in appearance (hence the brilliant colors used by the imperial family and the great clans). It was said to grant material prosperity as a reward (hence the Confucianist equation of wealth with goodness). In a word, it was considered *awesome*—something to fear, rather than love (hence the emphasis on unquestioning obedience to superiors, and the absence of words such as *compassion* from the Confucianist vocabulary). Such was the image of Heavenly Power that Confucianists presented to the common people. At the community level, it was shown in the courtroom treatment of complainants, witnesses, and the accused, not one of whom was allowed legal counsel or defense: All had to kneel on a hard floor (sometimes on chains) before the magistrate, who, as the emperor's representative in local government, had the right to extract testimony and confessions by torture—and, since under Chinese law no criminal could be sentenced until he had confessed, torture was the order of the day (hence the development of Chinese Torture). Because of centuries of this sort of intimidation, the majority of Chinese have tended to avoid whenever possible the workings of official government. Unfortunately, this Unwillingness to Openly Participate has allowed one tyrant after another—including those of the present totalitarian bureaucracy—to gain and maintain control of the nation.

Unlike the Confucianists, Taoists saw the Power of Heaven as both masculine and feminine, as symbolized by the Taoist *T'ai Chi*—the circle divided by a curved line into light and dark, or male and female, halves. Heavenly Power at work in the natural world, however—what Lao-tse called "The Mother of Ten Thousand Things"—has always been seen by Taoists as mostly feminine in its actions. It is gentle, like flowing water. It is humble and generous, like a fertile valley, feeding all who come to it. It is hidden, subtle, and mysterious, like a landscape glimpsed through mist. It takes no sides, grants no authority. It cannot be influenced or appeased by sacrifices and rituals. In dispensing justice, as in all things, it operates with a light touch, an invisible hand. As Lao-tse put it, "Heaven's net has wide meshes, but nothing slips through." Shying away from displays of arrogance and egotism, it communicates its deepest secrets not to high government officials, pompous scholars, or wealthy landowners, but to penniless monks, little children, animals, and "fools." If it can be said to be biased in any way, it is in favor of the humble, the weak, the small.

And that brings us back to Piglet.

As anyone can see, there are disadvantages to being a Very Small Animal. And one of those disadvantages is that bigger animals will try to take advantage of you. For example, let's recall Rabbit's famous Plan to Kidnap Baby Roo.

Practically as soon as Kanga and Roo arrived in the Forest, Rabbit decided that they ought to leave. We're not sure why—Rabbits are like that, sometimes. Anyway, Rabbit's plan involved—which in Rabbit terminology means *took advantage of*—Piglet and Pooh.

The idea was, Pooh would distract Kanga by talking to her, perhaps reciting some of his poetry (which ought to distract anyone). And—Ouch!

"That was uncalled for, Pooh."

"Was it?" asked Pooh. "I thought I heard you calling it."

And while Kanga's attention was diverted, Rabbit would place Piglet in her pouch—telling her it was Roo—and then run off with Roo. Afterward, when Kanga had discovered that Roo was missing . . . Then Rabbit, Pooh, and Piglet—all three of them, mind you—would say *"Aha!"* very loudly. As Rabbit explained it, a loud *"Aha!"* would mean that they had kidnapped Roo and would give him back only if Kanga were to promise to leave the Forest and never return. Kanga would grasp this meaning immediately, Rabbit said, as soon as Rabbit, Pooh, and Piglet (all three, mind you) said *"Aha!"* It went wrong—as Clever Plans by Rabbit always do—because first, Kangas think and respond differently from Rabbits; and second, as things turned out there was no loud, group-spoken *"Aha!"* to intimidate her, whether or not she would have understood what it was supposed to mean, anyway.

The first part of the plan went smoothly enough. They came across Kanga and Roo in the forest. Pooh distracted Kanga, Piglet jumped into Kanga's pouch, and Rabbit ran off with Roo. Unsuspecting Kanga bounced home with (bounce, bounce) Piglet (bounce, bounce, bounce). Pooh remained behind, practicing (thud) Kanga-jumps (crash). It wasn't until Kanga reached her house that the Trouble began:

Of course as soon as Kanga unbuttoned her pocket, she saw what had happened. Just for a moment, she thought she was frightened, and then she knew she wasn't; for she felt quite sure that Christopher Robin would never let any harm happen to Roo. So she said to herself, "If they are having a joke with me, I will have a joke with them."

"Now then, Roo, dear," she said as she took Piglet out of her pocket. "Bed-time."

"*Aha!*" said Piglet, as well as he could after his Terrifying Journey. But it wasn't a very good "*Aha!*" and Kanga didn't seem to understand what it meant.

"Bath first," said Kanga in a cheerful voice.

"*Aha!*" said Piglet again, looking round anxiously for the others. But the others weren't there. . . .

"I am not at all sure," said Kanga in a thoughtful voice, "that it wouldn't be a good idea to have a *cold* bath this evening. Would you like that, Roo, dear?"

Whether Roo would have or not, *Piglet* didn't.

But at last, the Cold Bath was over . . .

"Now," said Kanga, "there's your medicine, and then bed."

"W-w-what medicine?" said Piglet.

"To make you grow big and strong, dear. You don't want to grow up small and weak like Piglet, do you? Well, then!"

At that moment there was a knock at the door.

"Come in," said Kanga, and in came Christopher Robin.

"Christopher Robin, Christopher Robin!" cried Piglet. "Tell Kanga who I am! She keeps saying I'm Roo. I'm *not* Roo, am I?"

Christopher Robin looked at him very carefully, and shook his head.

"You can't be Roo," he said, "because I've just seen Roo playing in Rabbit's house."

"Well!" said Kanga. "Fancy that! Fancy my making a mistake like that."

"There you are!" said Piglet. "I told you so. I'm Piglet."

Christopher Robin shook his head again.

"Oh, you're not Piglet," he said. "I know Piglet well, and he's *quite* a different color."

Piglet began to say that this was because he had just had a bath, and then he thought that perhaps he wouldn't say that, and as he opened his mouth to say something else, Kanga slipped the medicine spoon in, and then patted him on the back and told him that it was really quite a nice taste when you got used to it.

What an ordeal. Well, that's what happens.

"Hey! What's dat noise outside?"

"Oh. Piglet's bodyguard. I'd forgotten you were here. It's some sort of siren, I think. Let me take a look . . . Yes—it's a police car."

"What?"

"That's strange. It's pulling up right in front of our house."

"Get away from dat window!"

"Of course. I didn't mean to—" Where'd he go?

Excuse me. I have to answer the door.

Little Piglet—held back by imaginings and fears, yearning to be Someone—is the last animal one might expect to accomplish anything of importance. And yet Piglet is the material from which heroes are made. Beneath the stalwart exterior of most any Courageous Rescuer, Gallant Fighter, or Great Achiever, a Piglet can be found, if one looks closely enough. So it has always been, as history clearly shows; and so, we're sure, it will always be.

In many ways, Piglet may appear the least

significant of the *Pooh* characters. Yet he is the only one of them to change, to grow, to become more than what he was in the first place. And in the end, he does this not by denying his smallness, but by applying it, for the good of others. He accomplishes what he does without accumulating a Large Ego; inside, he remains a Very Small Animal—but a different *kind* of Very Small Animal from what he was before.

For now, though, he hesitates and dreams. He has a good deal to go through before the Great Storm at the end of *The House at Pooh Corner*, which changes his life forever.

"How would *you* sum up Piglet's situation at this point, Pooh?"

"With a song," said Pooh.

"Wonderful. I was hoping you would."

"(er*hum*) . . ."

Animal so shy and small,
Dreaming you were Bold and Tall—
You hesitate, all sensitive,
Waiting for a chance to Live.

Time is swift, it races by;
Opportunities are born and die . . .
Still you wait and will not try—
A bird with wings who dares not
        rise and fly.

But that You you want to see
Is not <u>you</u>, and will never be.
No one else will ever do
The special things that wait
        inside of you.

You can be a guiding star,
If you make the most of Who You Are.
And the sensitivity
That you're now ashamed to see
Can be developed even more,
So you can find the hidden doors
To places no one's been before.
And the pride you'll feel inside
Is not the kind that makes you fall—
It's the kind that recognizes
The bigness found in being Small.

"Thank you, Pooh. That was excellent."

"Well," said Pooh, "it was better than I'd thought it would be."

Along the way to developing and applying
Sensitivity, there are things a Piglet needs to
watch out for. And one of them is found in the
next chapter.

THE EEYORE
EFFECT

"What's the matter, Piglet?" I asked.

"I was walking through the flowers just now," he said, "singing a little song, when Eeyore came up."

"Oh. Eeyore. What happened?"

"He said, 'Be careful, little Piglet—someone might pick you along with those pansies and put you in a vase on the mantelpiece. And *then* what would you do?' Then he walked away, chuckling to himself."

"Oh, don't mind Eeyore. He just likes to make others feel small, especially if they're smaller than he is, anyway. That makes him look big—he thinks."

"I wouldn't mind his being miserable by himself, if he enjoys it so. But why does he have to spread it around?"

There is something in each of us that wants us to be Unhappy. It creates in our imaginations problems that don't yet exist—quite often causing them to come true. It exaggerates problems that are already there. It reinforces low self-esteem and lack of respect for others. It destroys pride in workmanship, order, and cleanliness. It turns meetings into Confrontations, expectations into Dread, opportunities into Danger, stepping stones into Stumbling Blocks. It can be seen at work in grimaces and frowns, which pull the muscles of the face forward and down, speeding the aging process. It contaminates the mind behind the face with its negative energy and spreads outward, like a disease. And then it comes back, projected and reflected by other unhappy minds and faces. And on it goes.

Norman Cousins, editor of the *Saturday Review* for over thirty years, described the Eeyore Effect in an article he wrote following that magazine's demise:

Whatever success the *Saturday Review* may have

had was directly connected to its respect for the place of ideas and the arts in the life of the mind. This emphasis takes on special significance in the light of the sleaziness that has infected the national culture in recent years. There seems to be a fierce competition, especially in entertainment and publishing, to find ever-lower rungs on the ladder of taste. . . .

There is the curious notion that freedom is somehow synonymous with gutter jargon. At one time people who worked in the arts would boast to one another about their ability to communicate ideas that attacked social injustice and brutality. Now some of them seem to feel that they have struck a blow for humanity if only they can use enough four-letter words. . . .

The debasement of language not only reflects but produces a retreat from civility. The slightest disagreement has become an occasion for violent reactions. Television has educated an entire generation of Americans to believe that the normal way of reacting to a slight is by punching someone in the face.

The Eeyore Effect can be seen in every socially accepted negative phenomenon, such as the growing number of elderly young people whose

governing philosophy seems to be: It Won't Work,
So Why Try? Or in today's Death Camp Chic fash-
ions, and the popular Ugly-Skinny-Angry Look:

"Lobelia is dressed to kill or be killed in this
stunning black leather ensemble positively glowing
with terrorist charm. It's the look, the appeal, the
special touch that says Harley-Davidson. *Put away
that knife, Lobelia!* For heaven's sake! Somebody,
please—take it from her before she causes some
real harm."

The original Eeyore had at least a certain grim
sense of humor, a sort of funnyness-with-its-lights-
turned-out. Latter-day Eeyores seem to be missing
that. One thing they *do* have, however, is fear.
Eeyores are afraid—afraid to risk positive emotional expression, positive action, positive involve-
ment in anything beyond Ego. Those things are
stupid, they say, and they don't want to look stupid. (They don't seem to mind looking Paralyzed
with Fear—they just don't want to look *stupid*.)
Unfortunately for those around them, complaining
is one thing that Eeyores are not afraid to do. They
grudgingly carry their thimbles to the Fountain of
Life, then mumble and grumble that they weren't
given enough.

"Hallo, Eeyore," said Christopher Robin, as he opened the door and came out. "How are *you*?"

"It's snowing still," said Eeyore gloomily.

"So it is."

"*And* freezing."

"Is it?"

"Yes," said Eeyore. "However," he said, brightening up a little, "we haven't had an earthquake lately."

Eeyores are Realists, they say. But reality is what one makes it. And the more negative reality one nurtures and creates, the more of it one has. Eeyores see only what they want to . . . For example, never before in history has the individual had so much power, and so many opportunities to effect change. That assertion can be easily verified by taking a good look around. But the Eeyore Effect makes a great many people believe that they are powerless. And because they *believe* they're powerless, they are.

"I don't know how it is, Christopher Robin, but what with all this snow and one thing and another, not to mention icicles and such-like, it isn't so Hot in my field about three o'clock in the morning. . . ."

Without difficulties, life would be like a stream without rocks and curves—about as interesting as concrete. Without problems, there can be no personal growth, no group achievement, no progress for humanity. But what matters about

problems is what one *does* with them. Eeyores
don't overcome problems. No, it's the other way
around.

"And I said to myself: The others will be sorry if
I'm getting myself all cold. They haven't got
Brains, any of them, only grey fluff that's blown
into their heads by mistake, and they don't Think,
but if it goes on snowing for another six weeks or
so, one of them will begin to say to himself: 'Eeyore can't be so very much too Hot about three
o'clock in the morning.' And then it will Get
About. And they'll be Sorry."

Eeyores, in other words, are Whiners. They
believe the negative but not the positive and are
so obsessed with What's Wrong that the Good
Things in Life pass them by unnoticed. Are they
the ones, then, to give us an accurate account of

what life is about? If the universe were governed
by the Eeyore Attitude, the whole thing would
have collapsed eons ago. Everything in creation,
from migrating hummingbirds to spinning planets,
operates on the belief that It Can Be Done. To
quote William Blake, "If the Sun and Moon should
Doubt / They'd immediately Go Out."

Therefore, no society that wants to last is
going to be guided by Eeyores. For Eeyores sneer
at the very things that are needed most for survival
and prosperity. As Lao-tse wrote:

> When they hear of the Way,
> The highest minds practice it;
> The average minds think about it
> And try it now and then;
> The lowest minds laugh at it.
> If they did not laugh at it,
> It would not be the Way.

Pardon me a moment. This letter just arrived.

"Fan mail for Pooh, I suppose," said Piglet
enviously.

"For me?" said Pooh, waking up suddenly.

"No, it's . . . Hmm. I'll read it to you."

"Dear Sir:

"It has come to my attention that in your trifling book, *The Tao of Pooh*, you fail to mention a single positive attribute of that most charming of the A. A. Milne characters. I refer, of course, to the loveable ~~EOR~~ Eeyore.

"It is beyond my understanding how anyone could overlook the merits of the affable, debonair, and instigorating ~~EOR~~ Eeyore. His wit and wisdom can serve as an example to all in these dark days that envelop us."

"Dark?" said Pooh, looking out the window. "Where?"

"That's just a figure of speech, Pooh."

"Oh. One of those."

"He must have been in the dark when he *wrote* it," said Piglet, studying the letter.

"Do you mean the writing? It is pretty awful. But to continue . . ."

"Yes, in these times of tedium and ineptitude, it is refreshing—and encouraging—to know that there exists such a valuable, admirable, and *humble* animal as ~~EOR~~ Eeyore.

"A Friend

"P.S. Don't do it again."

Well, now we've heard from—er, whoever it was who sent this letter. I have a feeling that we'll hear from him again.

Let's look at some Eeyores Around Us. We will begin with what we call the Negative News Media. As Henry David Thoreau wrote, in *Walden*:

> I am sure that I never read any memorable news in a newspaper. If we read of one man robbed, or murdered, or killed by accident, or one house burned, or one vessel wrecked, or one steamboat blown up, or one cow run over on the Western Railroad, or one mad dog killed, or one lot of grasshoppers in the winter—we never need read of another. One is enough.

Today, thanks to the Negative News Media, we are overinformed about problems we can do little or nothing about. Despite the great fanfare made about these problems, few of them have much of anything to do with our lives. When it comes to those that *do*—such as the matter of what the local Nuclear Power Plant is doing to our health—the media are quite often silent. Strange. The Negative News Media rarely tell us of problems we can do something about, and never tell us what we can do about them. That would give us an unfair advantage, we suppose.

The Negative News Media sneer at everything and everyone, and call that Objectivity. Although there are courageous, noble-minded investigators and communicators in the news business, all too many of the rest behave like Peeping Toms with notebooks and cameras, who seem more interested in destroying heroes than in exposing villains. If the media build up some individuals in the public eye, it seems to be for the purpose of rubbing their remains in the public eye later on, in order to sell automobiles and toothpaste.

The heroes have flaws, we're told. Like Tigger, they can climb up but not down; their tails get in the way. So-and-So is just an ordinary man, after all. (That's a crime?) Such-and-Such is a crook. For some reason, however, the negative newsmongers tend to ignore the doings of the Biggest Crooks in the Highest Places—the ones who cause the greatest damage. Last month's Admirable People are now in disgrace and will quickly fade from sight. A new set will pop up in the latest broadcast or magazine issue, like targets in a shooting gallery. They in turn will be gunned down, and so on. The engineering of this process reminds us of some other words of William Blake: "A Truth that's told with bad intent / Beats all the Lies you can invent."

In reality, heroes are heroic because they, despite their weaknesses—and sometimes *because of* them—do great things. If they were perfect, they wouldn't be here in earth's classroom. Their strengths and weaknesses *could* be presented in an objective manner, for the enlightenment of others. But that's not what the Negative News Media do. Instead, they focus on the flaws in the most sensational manner, in order to make themselves wealthy. Who is going to take a chance at doing anything more than the mediocre, and help others to do the same, knowing that the Negative News Media are awaiting an opportunity to bring him crashing to the ground before an audience of millions?

Just as important, what effect does this constant character assassination have on that audience itself? To quote further from Henry David Thoreau . . .

If I am to be a thoroughfare, I prefer that it be of the mountain brooks, the Parnassian streams, and not the town sewers. There is inspiration, that gossip which comes to the ear of the attentive mind from the courts of heaven. There is the profane and stale revelation of the barroom and the police court. The same ear is fitted to receive both communications. . . . We should treat our minds, that is, ourselves, as innocent and ingenuous children, whose guardians we are, and be careful what objects and what subjects we thrust on their attention. Read not the *Times*. Read the Eternities.

Oops. Here he comes.

"Has anybody heard the news?" asked Eeyore, walking gloomily into the room.

"What is it now?" said I.

"Disaster. Horrendous, unspeakable *disaster*."

"I thought that was yesterday. Or the day before."

"It's in all the papers," said Eeyore, ignoring me as best he could.

"At what time does the earth explode?" I inquired, turning to look at the clock.

"Very amusing," said Eeyore. "In a pathetic sort of way."

"And when," I asked, "is the sun going dead?"

"Ha, ha. It's just what you *would* say. The sun going dead. Only don't blame me if it doesn't."

"All right, I won't. But I might blame you if it *does*."

All this about newspapers, gossip, and such brings us to those classic Eeyore killjoys and spoil-sports known as The Critics. You know what they are, whether they be professional Reputation Smashers or the Old Grump next door. If you sing, they can sing better (even though they can't sing). If you dance, they can dance better (even though they can't dance). If you direct a theater production, they can direct better (even though they can't direct). Whatever you do, they can do it better, even though they can't do it as well as you can. And since they can't *do* it as well as you, it shouldn't be particularly surprising if they don't accurately *judge* it. Whether in condemning Works of Genius or in praising the Truly Awful, The Critics tend to be wrong a disturbingly large amount of the time. Yet they can have tremendous influence, just the same. And that influence is responsible for the tragic loss of much that would have been of benefit to the world.

Chuang-tse described the limitations of The Critics in his story about a know-it-all quail:

There is a great bird known as the P'eng. Its back appears as broad as a mountain range; its wings are like clouds across the sky. It rises up like a whirlwind until it breaks through the high mist and soars into the infinite blue.

As it glides effortlessly along on its journey to the sea, a quail in the marsh looks up at it and laughs. "What does that bird think it's doing?" says the quail. "I jump up and fly a few feet; then I come down and flutter from here to there in the bushes. *That* is what flying is for! Who is that creature trying to fool?"

. . . So it is that the knowledge of the small-minded cannot reach to that which is great, just as the experience of a few years cannot equal that of many. The mushroom of a morning knows not what takes place at the end of the month; the short-lived cicada has no awareness of what happens in the seasons beyond.

Our favorite story about The Critics was told to us a few years ago by someone-or-other, who'd heard it who-knows-where:

While traveling separately through the country-side late one afternoon, a Hindu, a Rabbi, and a

Critic were caught in the same area by a terrific thunderstorm. They sought shelter at a nearby farmhouse.

"That storm will be raging for hours," the farmer told them. "You'd better stay here for the night. The problem is, there's only room enough for two of you. One of you'll have to sleep in the barn."

"I'll be the one," said the Hindu. "A little hardship is nothing to me." He went out to the barn.

A few minutes later, there was a knock at the door. It was the Hindu. "I'm sorry," he told the others, "but there is a cow in the barn. According to my religion, cows are sacred, and one must not intrude into their space."

"Don't worry," said the Rabbi. "Make yourself comfortable here. I'll go to sleep in the barn." He went out to the barn.

A few minutes later, there was a knock at the door. It was the Rabbi. "I hate to be a bother," he said, "but there is a pig in the barn. In my religion, pigs are considered unclean. I wouldn't feel comfortable sharing my sleeping quarters with a pig."

"Oh, all right," said the Critic. "*I'll* go sleep in the barn." He went out to the barn.

A few minutes later, there was a knock at the door. It was the cow and the pig.

The Critics can be pretty intimidating, all right. One can't do or say much of anything without fear of offending this particular—*very* particular—type of Eeyore. If you do or say the wrong thing (or the right thing), you may find yourself ostracized. But being Ostracized by Eeyores has its advantages. At least you don't have to associate with—

"Ostrich-sized?" said Pooh. "How can you be ostrich-sized? Unless you're an ostrich."

"No, not ostrich-sized. Ostracized."

"That's rather large, isn't it?" said Piglet. "They're such very big birds."

"No—not *ostrich*-sized. *Ostracized.*"

"They *are* big birds," said Owl.

"Now look here, all of you—"

"In fact, the male of the genus *Struthio* can attain a height of eight feet and a weight of three hundred pounds. As one might imagine, they can be quite dangerous when angered, and—"

Excuse me while I take this material into another room.

It was the first party to which Roo had ever been, and he was very excited. As soon as ever they had sat down he began to talk.

"Hallo, Pooh!" he squeaked.

"Hallo, Roo!" said Pooh.

Roo jumped up and down in his seat for a little while and then began again.

"Hallo, Piglet!" he squeaked.

Piglet waved a paw at him, being too busy to say anything.

"Hallo, Eeyore!" said Roo.

Eeyore nodded gloomily at him. "It will rain soon, you see if it doesn't."

Next we come to the Educator Eeyores, whose idea of teaching is *impress the maximum number of Unpleasant Things upon children at the minimum possible age.* Perhaps in the past these Eeyores were stepped on once too often by the Heel of Fortune and now want to take out their frustrations on people smaller than they are. Perhaps they truly believe that their approach to teaching is the best (despite the fact that few of their graduating students can even spell, or punctuate a sentence). We don't know. But we do know that their approach to education works against natural laws at practically every step of the way.

Mentally, emotionally, and physically, the human being is designed for a long childhood, followed by a short adolescence and then adulthood—the state of responsible, self-reliant wholeness. What we see children experiencing now, however, is an ever-shorter childhood, followed by a premature, prolonged adolescence from which ever fewer seem to be emerging.

Rather than help children develop the abilities needed to overcome the difficulties immediately confronting them, in the natural order in which they need to develop them, the Eeyore Educational System (with a good deal of help from parents and the entertainment industry) is forcing too much inappropriate information on them too soon, concerning—and causing—problems they can do nothing about. Then the children get stuck.

In response to the declining Test Scores of recent years, the educational system has brought in vastly expensive *machines* to do the teaching— a sign of trouble if there ever was one. Learn to write from a computer, and so on. (Of course, it *could* have brought in people who knew how to write, or whatever, to teach how to write, or whatever—on a volunteer basis, if necessary. But that would have been too simple, we suppose. Cheating, almost.) Now this costly Teaching Technology is bankrupting the system. So, in order to Cut Costs, the Eeyores are eliminating what *they* consider unnecessary classes—Art, Creative Writing, Drama, and so on—classes that help students observe, reason, and communicate, as well as keep their spirits and the right sides of their brains alive.

The Eeyore Educational System sees childhood as a waste of time, a luxury that society cannot afford. Its response to the problems of vanishing childhood is to speed up the process—give the students more information, give it to them at a faster rate, and give it to them sooner. Put children in school at the earliest age possible; load them down with homework; take away their time, their creativity, their play, their power; then plug them into machines. That'll whip them into shape. Well, it'll whip them, anyway.

Over two thousand years ago, Chuang-tse described a similar situation:

> The ancient emperor Shun encouraged rivalry in the minds of the people. Children were born the usual number of months after conception; but five months after that, they were being taught to converse. Soon they were calling people by their titles and personal names. Then men began to die while still young. . . .

> This governing provided order in name only. In reality, it produced chaos. It ran contrary to the light of the sun and the moon, brought harm to the mountains and rivers, and poisoned the fruit of the four seasons. It proved more deadly than the sting of a scorpion, or the bite of a dangerous beast.

The more that children are Educated by Eeyores, the more problems they develop. And the more problems they develop, the more the Eeyores insist on Educating them, at an ever-earlier age. The Educator Eeyores' answer to the problems that the Eeyores create is: Crack Down. The children's response is: Crack Up.

Piglet had got up early that morning to pick himself a bunch of violets; and when he had picked them and put them in a pot in the middle of his house, it suddenly came over him that nobody had ever picked Eeyore a bunch of violets, and the more he thought of this, the more he thought how sad it was to be an Animal who had never had a bunch of violets picked for him. So he hurried out again, saying to himself, "Eeyore, Violets," and then "Violets, Eeyore," in case he forgot, because it was that sort of day, and he picked a large bunch and trotted along, smelling them, and feeling very happy, until he came to the place where Eeyore was.

"Oh, Eeyore," began Piglet a little nervously, because Eeyore was busy.

Eeyore put out a paw and waved him away.

"Tomorrow," said Eeyore. "Or the next day."

Like the Iron Fist educators just mentioned, the following Eeyores work against natural laws and then complain about the results. In their behavior, they might be said to personify the opposite of the Taoist belief that the masculine and feminine earth energies need to be kept in balance, and that when the masculine is excessive the feminine needs to be advanced.

The rather Severe people we're thinking of might be called the Eeyore Amazons. They are emotionally descended from the Puritans—those grim souls who considered femininity No Good, along with art, music, dancing, singing, the natural world, and practically everything else that makes life enjoyable. As do a number of other people (us included), the Eeyore Amazons call themselves feminists. But the word doesn't quite fit them, somehow. They don't like femininity. Instead, they covet masculinity. Strange. Very strange.

Rather like certain joggers who are so automobile-oriented that they run on asphalt highways, gulping down noxious gases with every breath, the

Eeyore Amazons are so masculinity-oriented that they think of success, power, and all that in aggressive, combative masculine terms.

And so, just when a good many of us men have discarded earth-family-and-society-damaging *machismo*, along come the Eeyore Amazons, cursing and plundering like pirates in a bad Hollywood movie. Not exactly what we would call Advancing the Feminine. Yet even as they imitate and increase the worst sort of masculine energy, they denounce practically everything they dislike as masculine and a threat—to the extent of seeing masculinity and threats that aren't there. Stranger and stranger.

For example, the Amazons want to eliminate what they call the "masculine" (neutral) nouns, pronouns, and adjectives of the English language because, they say, these words are demeaning to women. Then they substitute words that are demeaning to everyone.

First, they made us change *chairman* to *chairperson*—which meant the same thing as *chairman*, only it was harder to say, longer to write, and just a bit silly. After a while, recognizing that *chairperson* was indeed rather awkward and stupid, they made us change it to *chair*. You know what a chair is. It's a thing. You sit on it.

So now Plain English has been turned into patronizing Lawyer-Politicianese . . .

> If a person does not keep pace with his or her companions, perhaps it is because he or she hears a different drummer [or drummerette?]. Let him, or her, step to the music which he, or she, hears, however measured or far away.

. . . and equally nonsensical Pluralspeak:

> If a person does not keep pace with their companions, perhaps it is because they hear a different drummer.

For a classic example of what Eeyore Politicizing can do to a language, here's a not-so-brief-anymore passage from the "improved" Oregon Revised Statutes—one of many such passages rewritten to avoid "masculine" terms and voted into law:

> (a) When owned or leased by a farmer and used in transporting the farmer's own agricultural commodities, agricultural products or livestock . . . that were originally grown or raised by the farmer on the farm of the farmer, or when used in any transportation which is incidental to the regular operation of the farm of the farmer, or

when used to transport supplies, equipment or materials to the farm of the farmer that are consumed or used on the farm of the farmer.

When all the books and so on have been censored and rewritten to suit the Eeyore Amazons, precisely what will have been accomplished? And why are *words* so important to them, anyway? For example, if they marry, they reject their husbands' family names. These names are paternal and are therefore symbols of "male chauvinism," they say. So they keep their unmarried names—which came from their fathers. (And their fathers were strong advocates of women's rights?)

Behind their antimasculine words, it's Overmasculinity as Usual, as the Eeyore Amazons imitate the lowest sort of masculine behavior and further the very energy they criticize. They break up Men's Clubs, which, they say, mean discrimination. Then they establish Women's Clubs, in which no men are allowed. They accuse men of being Sexists. Then they behave like Sexists. They say they want Sensitive Men. When they encounter such men, they shove them about. To put it plainly, *their* New Woman wants to be like the Old Man. And maybe even worse.

In a world that's practically screaming for relief from the Heavy Hand of Hypermasculinity, the Eeyore Amazons give us More of the Same. Who needs it? Countering Hypermasculinity with Hypermasculinity is rather like dousing a fire by pouring gasoline on it. You can't *beat* sensitivity into people. But you can beat it out of them.

Into what sort of future, and what sort of world, are the Eeyore Amazons pushing us? Where is respect for the feminine going? As anyone can see, women are being Used and Abused more than ever. Never have they been portrayed so demeaningly in movies, television shows, magazines, and books. And, according to statistics, the feminine side of the work force is not being paid as much for its efforts as it was twenty years ago. The influence of the Eeyore Amazons may not exactly be setting femininity Free, but it *is* making it Remarkably Cheap.

If truth be told, respect for the feminine is sinking like the *Titanic*—and, consequently, so is the state of the earth, the family, and society. The Eeyore Amazons blame men for all this. They might be wiser to blame misguided, excessive masculine energy—including that which they are advancing.

When the original *Titanic* went down, it was Women and Children First into the lifeboats. Now it's Women and Children Last. As a young man explained to us after a particularly nasty remark to his secretary, "We don't have to be nice to them anymore."

As do Eeyores in general, the Eeyore Amazons want men to stop being Chivalrous (not that many are now, anyway). Chivalry is Patronizing and Demeaning to Women, they say. But is it? And is chivalry limited to the behavior of men toward women? Whether of the European or the Asian variety, the code of chivalry makes kindness, consideration, and respect fashionable, and makes it admirable and desirable for the advantaged to assist the disadvantaged. Without chivalry, it's Claw and Fang, Might Makes Right, Kill or Be Killed. So we, along with past Taoist writers, knights-errant, and forest outlaws, would say: If you do away with chivalry, and do away with the feminine, Watch Out.

To close this chapter, we would like to quote from *Hope Against Hope: A Memoir*, in which Nadezhda Mandelstam described the Eeyore Effect at work in Stalinist Russia. Unfortunately, the principle involved is not limited to another society at another time, but is universal and ever-present:

There were once many kind people, and even un-
kind ones pretended to be good because that was
the thing to do. Such pretense was the source
of the hypocrisy and dishonesty so much exposed
in the realist literature at the end of the last
century. The unexpected result of this kind of
critical writing was that kind people disappeared.
Kindness is not, after all, an inborn quality—it has
to be cultivated, and this only happens when it is
in demand. For our generation, kindness was an
old-fashioned, vanished quality, and its exponents
were as extinct as the mammoth. Everything we
have seen in our times—the . . . class warfare, the
constant "unmasking" of people, the search for an
ulterior motive behind every action—all this has
taught us to be anything you like except kind.

How can one begin to overcome the Eeyore
Within, and thereby begin to counteract the Eeyore Effect? We will get to that in a moment. But
first . . .

THE TIGGER TENDENCY

It seems appropriate to begin this chapter with the Chinese story of "The Foolhardy Tiger":

A large tiger was swaggering through the forest. Above his head, a small bird danced from branch to branch, singing. The tiger stopped and watched him. Then he called out:

"What do you have to dance and sing about, you puny being? I am a thousand times larger than you. I can crush you in one paw, without even trying!"

"Can you do this?" replied the bird, hopping lightly from one branch to another.

"Of course I can!" roared the tiger. "Anything *you*

can do, I can do better!" He leaped onto the
trunk, climbed high into the tree, then jumped
out onto a branch. With a loud *crack*, it broke
beneath his weight. So did the branches below it,
all the way down. Ever so slowly, the bruised,
rumpled tiger rose to his feet and staggered away.

Limping out of the woods, the tiger came to the
edge of a field. There he saw a small, furry animal
with weak eyes and funny-looking feet. At least,
that's how they seemed to the tiger, who roared
with laughter, forgetting his pain.

"What are you laughing at?" asked the mole, looking up at him.

"What odd little feet!" laughed the tiger. "And
such weak little eyes!"

"I can see what I need to see," replied the mole.
"and I can go where I need to go."

"Ho, ho, ho!" laughed the tiger. "I can do both of
those things much better than you!"

"All right," said the mole. "Let's see you get past
all those workers out there in the field." He disappeared down a hole, and shortly popped up from
another hole beyond the farthest field hand.

"Here I come!" whooped the tiger, as he bounded into the field.

How the workers shouted! What heavy tools they swung! What large rocks they threw! The scarred, battered tiger stumbled back the way he had come, barely escaping with his life.

After a while, he came to a swamp. And there he noticed a tiny, slow-moving creature with a curly shell on his back. "What a useless little thing!" exclaimed the tiger. "No legs at all!"

"What do I need legs for?" asked the snail. "There are many places legs cannot go."

"*Where?*" asked the incredulous tiger.

"Across this swamp, for example," replied the snail.

"Nonsense!" thundered the tiger. "I can cross it in an instant, by jumping from log to log!" And without a moment's hesitation, he leaped for the nearest log. Unfortunately, he was too heavy for that sort of thing, and fell short.

The snail slid slowly across on the grasses of the swamp, leaving the struggling tiger far behind.

"Talking is one thing," he remarked to himself. "*Doing* is another."

In this chapter, we look at Eeyore's Opposite—an animal who believes in *everything* and believes that everything is Something He Can Do. All things are possible to a Tigger, at least until he tries them.

"How did you get there, Roo?" asked Piglet.

"On Tigger's back! And Tiggers can't climb downwards, because their tails get in the way, only upwards, and Tigger forgot about that when we started, and he's only just remembered. So we've got to stay here for ever and ever—unless we go higher. What did you say, Tigger? Oh, Tigger says if we go higher we shan't be able to see Piglet's house so well, so we're going to stop here."

As anyone who's been around one knows, Tiggers are first-rate at starting things, but are not very good at completing them. Life is always greener elsewhere to a Tigger once he's started something, and the Endless Possibilities constantly beckon—especially when he gets himself into a difficult situation, which is one thing Tiggers do quite easily.

. . . Tigger was holding on to the branch and saying to himself: "[Jumping down]'s all very well for Jumping Animals like Kangas, but it's quite different for Swimming Animals like Tiggers." And he thought of himself floating on his back down a river, or striking out from one island to another, and he felt that that was really the life for a Tigger.

"Come along," called Christopher Robin. "You'll be all right."

"Just wait a moment," said Tigger nervously. . . .

"Come on, it's easy!" squeaked Roo. And suddenly Tigger found how easy it was.

"Ow!" he shouted as the tree flew past him.

There's nothing wrong with being an Enthusiast. If it were not for enthusiasts, there would be
no Major Advances in life, and very little excitement. But enthusiasts are more than Tiggers. They
soon become well enough acquainted with whatever they're enthusiastic about to know when not
to put their foot in it. Tigger is an *over*enthusiast.
(And what *he* accomplishes is anybody's guess.)

In *The House at Pooh Corner*, Piglet described Tigger as "a Very Bouncy Animal, with a
way of saying How-do-you-do, which always left
your ears full of sand, even after Kanga had said,
'Gently, Tigger dear,' and had helped you up
again." Rabbit described him as "the sort of Tigger
who was always in front when you were showing
him the way anywhere, and was generally out of

sight when at last you came to the place and said
proudly 'Here we are!' " Alexander Pope described
him quite nicely when he wrote: "Some people
never learn anything because they understand everything too quickly." A psychiatrist might describe him as "an impulse-driven personality." We
would describe him as an animal with a whim of
iron and the inner discipline of mush.

While the Teachings of the West tend to encourage Tigger's sort of behavior, the Teachings of
the East contain many cautions against it. In the
Tao Te Ching, for example, we find:

> *High winds do not blow all morning;*
> *Heavy rain does not fall all day.*
> *Are not these made by heaven and earth?*
> *If the power of heaven and earth*
> *Cannot make violent activity last,*
> *How can you?*
>
> •   •   •
>
> *Standing on tiptoe, one is unsteady.*
> *Taking long steps, one quickly tires.*
> *Showing off, one shows unenlightenment.*
> *Displaying self-righteousness, one reveals vanity.*
> *Praising the self, one earns no respect.*
> *Exaggerating achievements, one cannot long*
>   *endure.*
> *Followers of the Way consider these*

Extra food, unnecessary baggage.
They bring no happiness.
Therefore, followers of the Way
Avoid them.

● ● ●

Do not conquer the world with force,
For force only causes resistance.
Thorns spring up when an army passes.
Years of misery follow a great victory.
Do only what needs to be done,
Without using violence.

● ● ●

It is not wise to dash about.
Shortening the breath causes stress.
Use too much energy, and
You will soon be exhausted.
That is not the Natural Way.
Whatever works against Tao
Will not last long.

"Going out, are you, Tigger?"

"Yes," he replied. "Roo and I are going on a picnic. I'm bringing the sandwiches."

"Oh? What's in that one?"

"Peanut butter, onions, mustard, and cheese."

"Oh. I . . . Er . . ."

"Is anything the matter?" asked Tigger. "You've gone green."

"No, it's nothing . . . Nothing at all. I'll be all right. I hope you're not going far."

"Why?" asked Tigger.

"Oh, just in case we have to bring Roo back suddenly."

"What for?"

"Nothing, nothing. Run along and enjoy yourselves. While you can."

Well, it takes all kinds to make a mess.

The West is full of Tiggers—restless seekers of instant gratification, larger-than-life overachievers. The West idolizes them because they're Bouncy and Exciting. Maybe even a bit *too* exciting. And they're becoming more exciting all the time. It seems that it's no longer adequate to be a True Individual, or even a Hero; now one needs to be some sort of Superman, living an overinflated life punctuated (in true Tigger fashion) with exclamation marks. *Faster than a speeding bullet! More powerful than a locomotive! Able to leap tall buildings in a single bound!* This is the age of Supereverything—Superstar, Superathlete, Supercoach, Superpolitician, even Superbusinessman: *Faster than a speeding ticket! More powerful than a profit motive! Able to lease tall buildings in a single day!*

Tiggers are not necessarily what they seem, however. While they may appear to be self-propelled, they are in reality jerked this way and that by whatever immediately appealing object or sensation catches their attention. And while Tiggers may appear energetic to the extreme, their love of ceaseless action and sensation is actually a form of spiritual laziness. Tiggers are not in control of their lives, as is clearly shown by their behavior.

Unfortunately, it is quite easy to be an impatient, inconsiderate, scatterbrained Tigger in a society that admires, encourages, and rewards impulsive behavior. Advertisements tell us to buy whatever-it-is and Spoil ourselves. An appropriate word, *spoil*. We deserve it, they say. (Maybe we do, but we'd like to think we're better than that.) Store layouts are carefully designed to encourage impulse buying. Movies, television shows, and magazines promote impulsive behavior of the most questionable kind, in the most flash-it-in-their-faces manner. Practically everything from hair-styles to life-styles is endorsed as some sort of drug to be taken Now for Instant Relief. If you have this model of automobile, this style of clothing, this shape of girlfriend, or this sort of romantic entanglement, you will be happy. You will be loved. You will be Somebody. Those who can't have such things are doomed to frustration. Those who *can* have them are doomed to the inevitable disappointment. As Oscar Wilde put it, "In the world there are only two tragedies. One is not getting what one wants and the other is getting it." We are reminded of the old Persian curse: "May your every desire be immediately fulfilled."

In chapter twelve of the *Tao Te Ching*, Lao-tse described what's wrong with Tigger's sensationalistic approach to life:

> *The five colors blind the eye.*
> *The five tones deafen the ear.*
> *The five flavors deaden the tongue.*
> *Racing and hunting madden the mind.*

While America is in many ways becoming Eeyore Country, in other ways it is turning into Tiggerland. A truly schizophrenic situation, one might say. The minds of American children are now so stressed and crippled by Tiggerish wham-bam Video Games, Television Shows, and Instant Left-Brain Computer Activities that many of them are unable to concentrate on anything for more than five minutes. As an ever-growing num-

ber of teachers are finding out, educating such
minds is impossible. If something can't be immediately grasped, they won't understand it. And if it
can be immediately grasped, they won't understand it, either—because Instant Information Ac-
cumulation is not *understanding*.

Perhaps today's children will be able to find
employment years from now; anyway—they may
be hired as technical laborers by the Chinese, Japanese, and Koreans, who will by then own just
about everything because their cultures far more
than ours encourage children to Focus the Mind.

The major lesson Tiggers need to learn is that
if they don't control their impulses, their impulses
will control them. No matter how much they do,
Tiggers are never satisfied because they don't
know the feeling of accomplishment that eventually comes when one persistently applies one's will
to the attaining of not-immediately-reachable goals.
The principle of this sort of achievement can be
illustrated by the following story by Chuang-tse:

K'ung Fu-tse and his followers were on their way
to the state of Ch'u. As they emerged from a forest, they came upon a hunchback catching cicadas
on the end of a stick as they flew by. "How skill-

ful!" exclaimed the Master, stopping to watch. "Sir, what is your method?"

"At first," the man answered, "I practiced balancing pellets on this stick. After five or six months, I could handle two until they never fell down. Then I failed with only a few of the insects. I went on to three pellets. After that, I missed only one cicada in ten. By the time I could manipulate five pellets, I was catching cicadas without effort.

"When I focus my attention, my body becomes no more than a stump, and my arm the branch of a tree. Heaven and earth are great, and the ten thousand things multiply around me—but I pay no attention to them, only to the wings of the cicadas. My mind does not waver; my body maintains its balance. With such an attitude, how can I fail?"

K'ung Fu-tse turned and said to his disciples, "Remember the saying of old: 'When one's will is not distracted, one's power is increased.' How well has this gentleman demonstrated the truth of that today!"

Something else that Tiggers need to learn is found in the Japanese story of "The Samurai and the Zen Master":

A certain samurai had a reputation for impatient and hot-tempered behavior. A Zen master, well known for his excellent cooking, decided that the warrior needed to be taught a lesson before he became any more dangerous. He invited the samurai to dinner.

The samurai arrived at the appointed time. The Zen master told him to make himself comfortable while he finished preparing the food. A long time passed. The samurai waited impatiently. After a while, he called out: "Zen Master—have you forgotten me?"

The Zen master came out of the kitchen. "I am very sorry," he said. "Dinner is taking longer to prepare than I had thought." He went back to the kitchen.

A long time passed. The samurai sat, growing hungrier by the minute. At last he called out, a little softer this time: "Zen Master—please. When will dinner be served?"

The Zen master came out of the kitchen. "I'm sorry. There has been a further delay. It won't be much longer." He went back to the kitchen.

A long time passed. Finally, the samurai couldn't endure the waiting any longer. He rose to his feet, chagrined and ravenously hungry. Just then, the Zen master entered the room with a tray of food. First he served *miso shiru* (soybean soup).

The samurai gratefully drank the soup, enchanted by its flavor. "Oh, Zen Master," he exclaimed, "this is the finest *miso shiru* I have ever tasted! You truly deserve your reputation as an expert cook!"

"It's nothing," replied the Zen master, modestly. "Only *miso shiru*."

The samurai set down his empty bowl. "Truly magical soup! What secret spices did you use to bring out the flavor?"

"Nothing special," the Zen master replied.

"No, no—I insist. The soup is extraordinarily delicious!"

"Well, there is one thing . . ."

"I knew it!" exclaimed the samurai, eagerly leaning forward. "There had to be *something* to make it taste so good! Tell me—what is it?"

The Zen master softly spoke: "It took *time*," he said.

"Tell me, Kanga—how has it been at your house since Tigger's been staying there?"

"Oh, it's been . . . *interesting.*"

"How do you mean?"

"Well, just yesterday morning, he knocked down the postman."

"Disgusting," said Owl, who had flown over to listen. "Absolutely disgusting."

"Why did he knock down the postman?"

"He thought he was taking something."

"Oh."

"Dis*gust*ing."

"You see, the postman carries a large sack—"

"Yes, yes. I hope Tigger apologized."

"He did. After I explained the situation."

"That's good."

"The postman was certainly decent about it."

"Oh? What did he say?"

"He said he'd been knocked down many a time by dogs—but never before by a *cat.*"

The final problem we might mention about the Tigger Tendency is that the worthwhile and important things in life—wisdom and happiness in particular—are simply not the sorts of things one can Chase After and Grab. They are instead the sorts of things that come to us where we are, if we let them—if we stop trying too hard and just let things happen as they need to. Tigger found this out in spite of himself when he discovered What Tiggers Like Best, in the second chapter of *The House at Pooh Corner*.

Tigger had just come to the Forest and needed breakfast. So Pooh offered him some honey—being sure to ask, of course, if Tiggers *like* honey. "They like everything," Tigger cheerfully assured him. But it didn't take Tigger long to realize that . . .

"Tiggers don't like honey."

"Oh!" said Pooh, and tried to make it sound Sad and Regretful. "I thought they liked everything."

"Everything except honey," said Tigger.

Pooh felt rather pleased about this, and said that, as soon as he had finished his own breakfast, he would take Tigger round to Piglet's house, and Tigger could try some of Piglet's haycorns.

"Thank you, Pooh," said Tigger, "because haycorns is really what Tiggers like best."

So they went to see Piglet.

"Hallo, Piglet. This is Tigger."

"Oh, is it?" said Piglet, and he edged round to the other side of the table. "I thought Tiggers were smaller than that."

"Not the big ones," said Tigger.

"They like haycorns," said Pooh, "so that's what we've come for, because poor Tigger hasn't had any breakfast yet."

Piglet pushed the bowl of haycorns towards Tigger, and said: "Help yourself," and then he got close up to Pooh and felt much braver, and said, "So you're Tigger? Well, well!" in a careless sort of voice. But Tigger said nothing because his mouth was full of haycorns . . .

After a long munching noise he said:

"Ee-ers o i a-ors."

And when Pooh and Piglet said "What?" he said "Skoos ee," and went outside for a moment.

When he came back he said firmly:

"Tiggers don't like haycorns."

"But you said they liked everything except honey," said Pooh.

"Everything except honey and haycorns," explained Tigger.

When he heard this, Pooh said, "Oh, I see!" and Piglet, who was rather glad that Tiggers didn't like haycorns, said, "What about thistles?"

"Thistles," said Tigger, "is what Tiggers like best."

So they went to see Eeyore.

"Hallo, Eeyore!" said Pooh. "This is Tigger."

"What is?" said Eeyore.

"This," explained Pooh and Piglet together, and Tigger smiled his happiest smile and said nothing.

Eeyore walked all round Tigger one way, and then turned and walked all round him the other way.

"What did you say it was?" he asked.

"Tigger."

"Ah!" said Eeyore.

"He's just come," explained Piglet.

"Ah!" said Eeyore again.

He thought for a long time and then said:

"When is he going?"

Almost immediately, as it turned out.

"What's the matter?" asked Pooh.

"*Hot!*" mumbled Tigger. . . .

"But you said," began Pooh—"you *said* that Tiggers liked everything except honey and haycorns."

"*And* thistles," said Tigger, who was now running round in circles with his tongue hanging out.

So they went to see *Kanga*. And when they had explained the situation to her, she kindly told Tigger to look in her cupboard to see what he'd like.

But the more Tigger put his nose into this and his

paw into that, the more things he found which Tiggers didn't like. And when he had found everything in the cupboard, and couldn't eat any of it, he said to Kanga, "What happens now?"

But Kanga and Christopher Robin and Piglet were all standing round Roo, watching him have his Extract of Malt. And Roo was saying, "Must I?" and Kanga was saying, "Now, Roo dear, you remember what you promised."

"What is it?" whispered Tigger to Piglet.

"His Strengthening Medicine," said Piglet. "He hates it."

So Tigger came closer, and he leant over the back of Roo's chair, and suddenly he put out his tongue, and took one large golollop, and, with a sudden jump of surprise, Kanga said, "Oh!" and then clutched at the spoon again just as it was disappearing, and pulled it safely back out of Tigger's mouth. But the Extract of Malt had gone.

"Tigger *dear!*" said Kanga.

"He's taken my medicine, he's taken my medicine, he's taken my medicine!" sang Roo happily, thinking it was a tremendous joke.

Then Tigger looked up at the ceiling, and closed his eyes, and his tongue went round and round his chops, in case he had left any outside, and a peaceful smile came over his face as he said, "So *that's* what Tiggers like!"

And so—

CRASH!!!!

"Tigger, help the man up. That's Piglet's bodyguard you just knocked over. I mean, his *former* bodyguard."

"He's gone to sleep," said Tigger.

"No, I think he's unconscious. That was a little rough, wasn't it?"

"I was in a hurry," explained Tigger. "He got in the way."

"He must have come back for something. That's strange. I thought he'd gotten just about everything he could. Well, he won't get away this time."

"You're sorry about hitting his head with the floor, aren't you, Tigger? That's good."

Excuse me while I call the police.

THINGS AS THEY
MIGHT BE

By and by Piglet woke up. As soon as he woke he said to himself, "Oh!" Then he said bravely, "Yes," and then, still more bravely, "Quite so." But he didn't feel very brave, for the word which was really jiggeting about in his brain was "Heffalumps."

What was a Heffalump like?

Was it Fierce?

Did it come when you whistled? And *how* did it come?

Was it Fond of Pigs at all?

If it was Fond of Pigs, did it make any difference *what sort of Pig*?

Supposing it was Fierce with Pigs, would it make
any difference *if the Pig had a grandfather called
TRESPASSERS WILLIAM*?

In this chapter, we come from the illusions of
Eeyore and Tigger to those of Piglet, and to illusions in general. To the Taoist, unhappiness is the
result of being guided by illusions—such as the
mistaken belief that man is something separate
from the natural world. Problems, be they eco-
nomical, ecological, or whatever, are caused by a
failure to see What's There. Unpleasant feelings
come from illusions: fear from What Might Be
(which hasn't happened yet), sadness from What
Might Have Been (which is not necessarily what
would have been), and so on. Piglets, living in fear
of What's Coming Next, What Can Go Wrong,
What If I Do Something Foolish, and such, cannot
enjoy and make the most of the present moment.
Later, they look back and realize that they didn't
live it. And that realization makes them feel more
inadequate than they already did. However, because of their sensitivities, their strong experience-
filing-and-recalling memories, and their cautious,
one-step-at-a-time natures, Piglets—far more than
Eeyores and Tiggers, Rabbits and Owls—have the

ability to rise to a challenge and accomplish the most difficult tasks, once interfering illusions have been cleared away.

We will begin our examination of illusions with three narratives concerning the Perception of Situations, which show that It All Depends on How One Looks at Things. The first is by the Taoist writer Lieh-tse:

> A man noticed that his axe was missing. Then he saw the neighbor's son pass by. The boy looked like a thief, walked like a thief, behaved like a thief. Later that day, the man found his axe where he had left it the day before. The next time he saw the neighbor's son, the boy looked, walked, and behaved like an honest, ordinary boy.

The second example is the Chinese story of "The Well by the Road":

> A man dug a well by the side of a road. For years afterward, grateful travelers talked of the Wonderful Well. But one night, a man fell into it and drowned. After that, people avoided the Dreadful Well. Later it was discovered that the victim was a drunken thief who had left the road to avoid being captured by the night patrol—only to fall into the Justice-Dispensing Well.

Same well; different views.

The third selection is from the writings of Chuang-tse:

> An archer competing for a clay vessel shoots effort-lessly, his skill and concentration unimpeded. If the prize is changed to a brass ornament, his hands begin to shake. If it is changed to gold, he squints as if he were going blind. His abilities do not deteriorate, but his belief in them does, as he allows the supposed value of an external reward to cloud his vision.

Unfortunately, even the wise can occasionally go wrong by misinterpreting what's in front of them. In the third chapter of *Winnie-the-Pooh*, for example, a certain Wise but Overstuffed Bear—

"*Who*'s Overstuffed?" said Pooh.

"All right, Pooh, you're not Overstuffed. You're Physically Superfluous."

"Oh, I wouldn't go *that* far," said Pooh modestly.

Anyway, Winnie-the-Pooh, whom most every-one calls Pooh, for short, was—

"No one calls me Pooh for Short," said Pooh. "Just Pooh."

Yes. All right . . . Winnie-the-Pooh, whom most everyone calls Just Pooh, was walking around and around in the snow near Piglet's house. When Piglet asked him what he was doing, he said he was Tracking something. He didn't know what. Possibly—just *possibly*, you know—it was a Woozle. Possibly it was more than that.

"It's a very funny thing," said Bear, "but there seem to be *two* animals now. This—whatever-it-was—has been joined by another—whatever-it-is—and the two of them are now proceeding in company. Would you mind coming with me, Piglet, in case they turn out to be Hostile Animals?"

And Piglet, who ought to have known better, didn't. We mean, he did. Join him, that is.

There was a small spinney of larch trees just here, and it seemed as if the two Woozles, if that is what they were, had been going round this spinney; so round this spinney went Pooh and Piglet after them; Piglet passing the time by telling Pooh what his Grandfather Trespassers W had done to Remove Stiffness after Tracking, and how his Grandfather Trespassers W had suffered in his later years from Shortness of Breath, and other matters of interest, and Pooh wondering what a Grandfather was like, and if perhaps this was Two Grandfathers they were after now, and, if so, whether he would be allowed to take one home and keep it, and what Christopher Robin would say. And still the tracks went on in front of them. . . .

Suddenly Winnie-the-Pooh stopped, and pointed excitedly in front of him. *"Look!"*

"What?" said Piglet, with a jump. And then, to show that he hadn't been frightened, he jumped up and down once or twice in an exercising sort of way.

"The tracks!" said Pooh. *"A third animal has joined the other two!"*

So—things were beginning to look Slightly Dangerous for Pooh and Piglet. But at least the third animal wasn't a Woozle. As Pooh pointed out, its prints were different from the first two sets. They were smaller.

So they went on, feeling just a little anxious now, in case the three animals in front of them were of Hostile Intent. . . . And then, all of a sudden, Winnie-the-Pooh stopped again, and licked the tip of his nose in a cooling manner, for he was feeling more hot and anxious than ever in his life before. *There were four animals in front of them!*

The suspense was becoming unbearable. No, that's not the word we want. What we mean is . . .

"I *think*," said Piglet, when he had licked the tip of his nose, too, and found that it brought very little comfort, "I *think* that I have just remem-

bered something. I have just remembered something that I forgot to do yesterday and shan't be
able to do tomorrow. So I suppose I really ought
to go back and do it now."

"We'll do it this afternoon, and I'll come with
you," said Pooh.

"It isn't the sort of thing you can do in the afternoon," said Piglet quickly. "It's a very particular
morning thing, that has to be done in the morning, and, if possible, between the hours of—What
would you say the time was?"

"About twelve," said Winnie-the-Pooh, looking at
the sun.

"Between, as I was saying, the hours of twelve
and twelve five. So, really, dear old Pooh, if you'll
excuse me—*What's that?*"

It was Christopher Robin, whistling to them
from the branches of a nearby tree. What a relief.

"Silly old Bear," he said, "what *were* you doing?
First you went round the spinney twice by yourself, and then Piglet ran after you and you went
round again together, and then you were just
going round a fourth time—"

Oh. So that's what it was. How embarrassing.

Speaking of snow, we might also mention the time that Pooh and Piglet were out on a walk and decided to build a house for Eeyore in a sheltered spot in the pine wood by Eeyore's Gloomy Place. Of course, they needed something to build it with. Sticks would work nicely.

"There was a heap of sticks on the other side of the wood," said Piglet. "I saw them. Lots and lots. All piled up."

So they took the pile of sticks and made a house for Eeyore. And later, when Eeyore couldn't find his pile of—that is, when he couldn't find his house, he and Christopher Robin went looking for it, and met Pooh and Piglet, and . . .

"*Where* did you say it was?" asked Pooh.

"Just here," said Eeyore.

"Made of sticks?"

"Yes."

"Oh!" said Piglet.

"What?" said Eeyore.

"I just said 'Oh!' " said Piglet nervously. And so as to seem quite at ease he hummed Tiddely-pom once or twice in a what-shall-we-do-now kind of way.

"You're sure it *was* a house?" said Pooh. "I mean, you're sure the house was just here?"

"Of course I am," said Eeyore. And he murmured to himself, "No brain at all some of them."

"Why, what's the matter, Pooh?" asked Christopher Robin.

"Well," said Pooh. . . . "The fact *is*," said Pooh . . . "Well, the fact *is*," said Pooh . . . "You see," said Pooh. . . . "It's like this," said Pooh, and something seemed to tell him that he wasn't explaining very well, and he nudged Piglet again.

"It's like this," said Piglet quickly. . . . "Only warmer," he added after deep thought.

"What's warmer?"

"The other side of the wood, where Eeyore's house is."

So they went there, and Eeyore found his house, and . . .

So they left him in it; and Christopher Robin went back to lunch with his friends Pooh and Piglet, and on the way they told him of the Awful Mistake they had made. And when he had finished laughing, they all sang the Outdoor Song for Snowy Weather the rest of the way home. . . .

How embarrassing.

"We're back," said Pooh.

"So you are. I was so busy writing that I didn't realize you'd gone."

"Piglet and I were just going over some Riddles," said Pooh. "Piglet has one for you."

"Very good, Piglet. What's your Riddle?"

"It's this," said Piglet. "What barks and has feathers?"

"Barks and has feathers? I . . . I don't know."

"A bird dog."

"Hmm."

"Is something wrong?" asked Piglet.

"All right, Piglet, here's one for you. What's the difference between a filing cabinet and a kangaroo?"

"I don't know," said Piglet.

"You don't? *You don't know the difference be-tween a filing cabinet and a kangaroo?*"

"No," said Piglet.

"Well, then, I won't let you file any of *my* papers."

Silence.

"I don't get it," said Pooh.

In addition to the common human tendency to misinterpret What's There—as demonstrated by sometimes-a-little-too-human Pooh and Piglet in the snow just now—we might mention the inclination of a good many people to fail to notice anything but the unusual, as can be illustrated by the Chinese story of "The Ox and the Rat":

Many years ago Buddha called twelve animals before him, and told them that he would name a year of the Chinese zodiac after each. The animals were very pleased. But then the question of order arose, and trouble began.

"I should be first," said the rat, "because of my intelligence."

"No, *I* should be first," said the ox. "Because of my size."

The two animals argued for some time about which was more important, intelligence or size. After a while, the rat fell silent. "All right," he said at last, "I admit that size is more important." "Good," said the ox. "It's settled." "Not so fast," said the rat. "My size is more impressive than yours." "*What?*" snorted the indignant ox. "How can you, a mere rodent, impress anyone with your size?" "Let us go before the people," replied the rat, "and let the opinion of the majority decide." "Ridiculous!" the ox exclaimed. "Why should we waste time on your nonsense? Anyone can see that—"

"Now, now," said Buddha. "Let's not argue about it any longer. Of course the rat is smaller than you are. But why not let the majority of the people decide? Whoever more impresses them with his size shall be declared the winner." The ox, certain of victory, agreed.

"Lord Buddha," said the rat. "With the consent of the ox, I wish to have one favor granted before we present ourselves. If I am truly as small as the ox insists I am, I should like to lessen my inevitable embarrassment. Therefore, I ask that you temporarily double my size."

Buddha asked the ox if he had any objections. "Of course not," the ox answered. "After all, how much difference could it make? I'd still be one hundred times bigger than he is!"

The ox and the rat, the rat now twice his ordinary size, went out and walked among the crowds. Everywhere they went, people exclaimed in amazement. "Look at the size of that rat!" they shouted. *"Look at that enormous rat!"* No one noticed the ox. Everyone had seen an ox before. There was nothing unusual about him.

And that is how the rat impressed the people with his size, and became the first animal in the Chinese zodiac.

"By the way, Piglet, I've been thinking about that sign by your house . . ."

"You mean 'TRESPASSERS W'?"

"Yes. That was your grandfather's name, you said."

"Yes—Trespassers William."

"Well, he must have been a rather large pig, to put up such a tall sign."

"Er . . . Well . . . He didn't put it up himself. A friend did it for him."

"A friend?"

"Yes, another sort of animal. A *tall* sort of animal."

"You mean, like a giraffe?"

"Yes, yes—a giraffe. That was it."

"It must have been an amusing friendship, a pig and a giraffe. I didn't know giraffes could be found around here."

"They can't," said Piglet. "Ordinarily. But this giraffe was over here on an Exchange Program."

"Oh? What did we send in exchange?"

"Er . . . A box of weasels."

"That doesn't sound like a very fair exchange."

"Well, it was a *large* box."

Yes, well . . . Speaking of Illusions, let's return to that subject. We believe there are a few things more to be said.

Although Illusions exist all over the world, the Industrial West seems to have more than a fair share of them. And the Illusions of the West— which of course by now have been exported to the East—deserve to be watched out for with special care. It seems rather ironic, somehow, that "realistic," "scientific" Western industrial society sneers at the relatively harmless myths and acquired beliefs of the native peoples of the world—a good many of which have at least some basis in fact—while perpetuating irrational beliefs and practices so dangerous that they are destroying the earth. And probably the most destructive of all the Illusions of the West is the superstitious notion that Technology will solve all our difficulties.

This Technology Worship could be said to have started in Western Europe in the 1500s or so, with Explorations and Expansions that led to the growth of Commercialism, which led to the Industrial Revolution of the 1700s. The rapid proliferation of Hungry Machines, and the accompanying breakneck exploitation of natural resources with which to feed them, quickly transformed rural, agricultural societies—"Good morning, Mrs. Witherspoon! What a lovely cow!"—into city and factory societies ("I certainly hope—gasp, wheeze—we don't run out of—cough—*coal* before the day is over!") and then into big city, big industry societies: "That's right, Inspector—*they stole everything that wasn't fastened to the floor!*" In the Victorian era, this Industrial Fanaticism was given a large boost by empire-and-opinion makers who believed that science could do anything, and that any opinions to the contrary were heresy.

But well before then, some similar pillage-the-earth-and-let's-have-no-nonsense-about-it nonsense had been exported from Europe to the New World. And with it came the absurd and groundless belief that money could buy happiness. It would have been rather surprising if such a belief had *not* arrived on these shores, considering that a good many of the earliest immigrants were debtors from English prisons, fur trappers, tobacco and cotton barons-to-be, and Puritan tradesmen. Such people tended to know enough about the natural world to exploit it, but not much more—if indeed they knew even that. The Puritans in particular knew next to nothing about how to get along in the North American forests, meadows, and mountains, and next to nothing about how to get along with the people who did. As the old saying puts it, "They fell first upon their knees, and then upon the Indians." And then upon the landscape. As Luther Standing Bear, chief of the Oglala Sioux, described the situation:

> We did not think of the great open plains, the beautiful rolling hills, and winding streams with

tangled growth, as "wild." Only to the white man
was nature a "wilderness" and only to him was the
land "infested" with "wild" animals and "savage"
people. To us it was tame. Earth was bountiful
and we were surrounded with the blessings of the
Great Mystery. Not until the hairy man from the
east came and with brutal frenzy heaped injustices
upon us and the families we loved was it "wild"
for us. When the very animals of the forest began
fleeing from his approach, then it was that for us
the "Wild West" began.

Today, thanks to this rather lopsided cultural
foundation, we live in what is commonly described
as a Materialistic Society. But that description is
in error. Ours is in reality an Abstract Value society—one in which things are not appreciated for
what they *are* so much as for what they *represent*.
If Western industrial society appreciated the Material World, there would be no junkyards, no
clearcut forests, no shoddily designed and manu-
factured products, no poisoned water sources, no
obese, fuel-guzzling automobiles, nor any of the
other horrors and eyesores that haunt us at every
turn. If ours were a materialistic society, we would
love the physical world—and we would know our
limits within it.

In truth, Western industrial society does not

even *notice* the Material World. It quickly discards it, leaves it to rust in the rain. The material world is Here and Now, and industrial society does not appreciate or pay attention to the Here and Now. It's too busy coveting and rushing after the There and Later On. As a result, it all too often fails to see what is right in front of it, and what's coming from that. It forgets where it has been; it does not know where it is going.

> "Going on an Expotition?" said Pooh eagerly. "I don't think I've ever been on one of those. Where are we going to on this Expotition?"
>
> "Expedition, silly old Bear. It's got an 'x' in it."
>
> "Oh!" said Pooh. "I know." But he didn't really.
>
> "We're going to discover the North Pole."
>
> "Oh!" said Pooh again. "What *is* the North Pole?" he asked.
>
> "It's just a thing you discover," said Christopher Robin carelessly, not being quite sure himself.

Perhaps the preceding glimpse at our historical conditioning can help to explain why Western

industrial society has such a poor record when it
comes to observing What's There. In our part of
the world, this unobservant tendency is displayed
in the most depressing manner whenever there's
an Election. For nearly thirty years now, the nation that was once the Light of the Free World
has been electing to the highest office in the land
a succession of Nightmare Clowns who lead us
deeper and deeper into darkness as they encourage
massive greed and corruption, run up multibillion-
dollar debts for future generations to pay, turn the
economy into jelly, refuse to take action necessary
to save what's left of the natural world ("More
studies are needed"), and threaten to blow up the
planet because some country somewhere isn't
doing what they think it ought to quickly enough—
all the while making remarks on the intelligence
level of "If you've seen one redwood tree, you've
seen them all."

And speaking of trees, if the majority of voters are not living in some sort of fantasy, why this
increasing tendency to talk about Protecting the
Environment while voting more than ever against
it? In a recent election in our once-almost-environ-
mentalist home state, for example, the majority
voted to allow one of the nation's most notoriously

unsafe and unnecessary nuclear power plants to continue operation despite its persistent violation of vital safety regulations; rejected a measure that would have restricted throwaway packaging; and turned down an honest, self-funded, pro-environment political candidate to re-elect a politician who for years has actively opposed the preservation of what little remains of the state's uncut forests, who supports the timber industry's policy of clear-cutting public lands and sending the logs overseas for processing, and who has annually appended to appropriations bills riders forbidding citizens from challenging old-growth timber sales in court. So much for Planet Earth.

The natural world is all right, voters across the country seem to be saying, as long as its preservation doesn't interfere with the process of destroying it to earn money. Let Someone Else pay for its protection. But, considering that less than 1 percent of American philanthropic giving goes to conservation, it would appear that Someone Else is just another fantasy.

"We're all going on an Expotition with Christopher Robin!"

"What is it when we're on it?"

"A sort of boat, I think," said Pooh.

"Oh! That sort."

"Yes. And we're going to discover a Pole or some-thing. Or was it a Mole? Anyhow we're going to discover it."

Unfortunately for our chances of survival and happiness, we in the West have inherited an Eey-ore version of religion, which denounces the world as an evil place whose ways are to be ignored by the wise, and an Eeyore sort of science, which sneers at anything beyond a mechanistic view of the earth—the secrets of which it attempts to sneak out of it bit by bit, for the purpose of manip-ulating the natural world. Is either of these Ways very likely to get us out of the mess we're in? Or to even help us see what's causing it?

Eeyore religion says that the earth isn't worth saving, anyway, and that when it comes to an end, the Faithful will be transported instantly to heaven. No problem. We'd like to see them ex-plain things to Saint Peter at the Gate, when he asks them what they did with the world that God entrusted to them. *That* might get a bit sticky.

Eeyore science, on the other hand, insists that Technology will rescue us from destruction—including the considerable destruction that Technology causes. When it tells us things like that, we can't help but wonder if it isn't trying to be some sort of religion itself. No, not a religion, exactly—some sort of *voodoo.*

"*Wunga wunga, moomba noonga*—Great Tin God, save us from hexachlorobenzene, ethylene dibromide, toxaphene, chlordane, parathion, and everything else you've given us that's gone wrong." Well, *wunga wunga,* everybody—and lots of luck!

"Oh! Piglet," said Pooh excitedly, "we're going on an Expotition, all of us, with things to eat. To discover something."

"To discover what?" said Piglet anxiously.

"Oh! just something."

"Nothing fierce?"

"Christopher Robin didn't say anything about fierce. He just said it had an 'x'."

"It isn't their necks I mind," said Piglet earnestly.
"It's their teeth. . . ."

The fearful fantasies we have inherited have
conditioned us to believe that we need to be protected from the natural world. Better Living
Through Heavy Industry, and so on. In reality, as
anyone ought to be able to see by now, the natural
world needs to be protected from us. Its wisdom
needs to be recognized, respected, and understood
by us, and not merely viewed through the dis-
torted lenses of our illusions about it. As Sir Arthur
Conan Doyle cautioned, through his character
Sherlock Holmes, "One's ideas must be as broad
as Nature if they are to interpret Nature," and
"When one tries to rise above Nature one is liable
to fall below it." Chuang-tse's words to that effect
have a timely ring:

When leaders pursue knowledge but do not follow
the Way, all who follow them become lost in confusion. How can I say this is so?

Much knowledge is applied in the making of bows,
crossbows, arrows, and slingshots, but the birds
in the air are disturbed and injured by it. Much
knowledge is used in making hooks, nets, and
other such devices, but the fish in the waters are

disturbed and injured by it. Much knowledge is utilized in the design and placement of traps, meshes, and snares, but the creatures of the ground are disturbed and injured by it.

As knowledge becomes increasingly clever, versatile, and artful, the people all around are disturbed and injured by it. They then struggle to grasp what they do not know, but make no attempt to grasp what they know already. They condemn the misunderstanding of others, but do not condemn their own. From this more confusion comes.

If the sun and moon lost their light, the mountains and rivers abandoned their vitality, and the four seasons came to an end, no insect or plant would retain its true nature. Yet this is the condition produced in men by an obsession for knowledge. Honesty and simplicity are overlooked, and restlessness is admired. Quiet, effortless action is forgotten, and loud quarreling is heard. Such is the nature of hunger for knowledge. Its noise throws the world into chaos.

We might add some other words by Chuang-tse:

Men honor what lies within the sphere of their

knowledge, but do not realize how dependent they are on what lies beyond it.

To illustrate the vital truth of that last statement, we have decided to give a very brief history of what we call Popular Radiation.

In the 1930s, as people were dying from the effects of radium-laced Health Tonics, the U.S. government established its first maximum level of tolerable exposure to radiation. Just in case, you know.

In the 1940s, following study of Hiroshima bombing victims, that level was halved. Just to be safe, you understand.

In the 1950s, in response to concern over nuclear-bomb-testing fallout, which seemed to be affecting some people in unpleasant ways, the maximum tolerable level was substantially lowered. Just as a precaution.

At the same time, however, utility company advertisements were extolling the charms of the newest form of power generation—"clean, safe" nuclear energy. Their billboards invited customers to "Take the Family to the Nuclear Power Park." X-ray machines were being used in shoe stores to examine children's feet. And people were having their supposedly-enlarged-but-actually-normal thymus glands irradiated. Like many exposed to radiation before them, a sizable number of these people developed cancer and died.

In the 1960s, more and more people came to suspect that they weren't being told the Whole Truth about this sort of thing. And then . . .

In the 1970s, researchers reported that Americans were being exposed to nine times more radiation from medical applications than from atmospheric nuclear fallout—which by then, due in part to studies of certain Nevada residents and military personnel, was being connected with all sorts of problems. In 1979, the Three Mile Island nuclear power facility broke down and irradiated the surrounding area.

In the 1980s, new data on the Hiroshima victims and their descendants showed that the risk of cancer from radiation was up to fifteen times greater than authorities had previously believed. Emissions from nuclear plants were linked with thyroid damage, miscarriages, and other health problems. And before the end of the decade, the Chernobyl nuclear facility, like Three Mile Island before it, had done what experts in the field had said it wouldn't do in a thousand years. Reports of

near-disasters at other plants were being leaked to
the press . . . So the "safe exposure" level was
lowered again. Not taking any chances.

At each step of the way, authorities assured
the public that the New Devices and New
Amounts of radiation were safe. And each time,
they were wrong.

Today the public is being captivated by com-
puters, word processors, and the like—whose cath-
ode ray tubes emit X-ray radiation, and whose
circuits and display terminals produce strong electromagnetic fields. They're perfectly safe, authorities assure us. And if any difficulties *should* happen
to develop, we will certainly be notified later on.

The latest Popular Radiation device is the Mi-
crowave Oven, which bombards food with high-
frequency electromagnetic radiation, irritating it
until it heats up. This sort of Perversion of Nature
is perfectly safe, authorities insist—if it weren't,
the Wonderful Machines wouldn't be on the market. Maybe the authorities are correct this time,
just for once. On the other hand, maybe they're
not.

As soon as he had finished his lunch Christopher
Robin whispered to Rabbit, and Rabbit said, "Yes,

yes, of course," and they walked a little way up the stream together.

"I didn't want the others to hear," said Christopher Robin.

"Quite so," said Rabbit, looking important.

"It's—I wondered—It's only—Rabbit, I suppose *you* don't know, What does the North Pole *look* like."

"Well," said Rabbit, stroking his whiskers. "Now you're asking me."

"I did know once, only I've sort of forgotten," said Christopher Robin carelessly.

"It's a funny thing," said Rabbit, "but I've sort of forgotten too, although I did know *once*."

"I suppose it's just a pole stuck in the ground?"

"Sure to be a pole," said Rabbit, "because of calling it a pole, and if it's a pole, well, I should think it would be sticking in the ground, shouldn't you, because there'd be nowhere else to stick it."

"Yes, that's what I thought."

"The only thing," said Rabbit, "is *where is it sticking?*"

"That's what we're looking for," said Christopher Robin.

"Say, Piglet—what's that at the window?"

"*It's the Heffalump!*" cried Piglet, jumping straight up in alarm.

"Oh—it's the garbageman, taking away the recycling. You didn't really think it was a Heffalump, did you?"

"No (pant, pant). Not (pant) really."

"Now, Piglet. What if it *had* been a Heffalump? What could he have done to you?"

"I don't know," squeaked Piglet. "But he might have thought of *something*."

"You don't even know what a Heffalump is, do you?"

"No . . . Not exactly."

"You don't even know if Heffalumps *exist*."

"Well, do they?"

"Not in this part of the world, anyway—not lurking about outside the window."

"Are you sure?"

"Absolutely. You won't find a Heffalump around

here any more than you'll find a giraffe putting up a sign by your house."

"Oh," said Piglet. "I see."

Where were we? Oh, yes—dangerous illusions. In his amazingly Taoist-like *Magical Child*, Joseph Chilton Pearce described our society's predicament this way:

> How do we believe that we can predict and control the natural forces of the universe? Through clever intellectual manipulations and tool usage. We accept this notion so completely because we have been conditioned to believe implicitly that only by so using our intelligence can we, in fact, survive nature. Interaction between the mind-brain and its source of information [the earth] has been rigorously, religiously denied by Western logic, if not *most* cultural logic. Interaction with the living earth would imply that the earth responded in kind, interacting with us. And the one cardinal rule of all classical Western academic belief . . . is that the mind has absolutely no relation to the world other than to be informed of that world through the senses and to make some sort of intelligent reaction to that information. This belief has automatically robbed us of personal power. Having no personal power to draw on, we are re-

duced to only one source of power: tool usage. And so, we have evolved a continuing body of knowledge concerning the employment, creation, enhancement, and service of tools. Our real criterion of value becomes the culture's body of knowledge offering or promising enhanced tool production, possible domination of nature, and so some security. *Potential is seen as an increase of tools*. [our emphasis] The training and education of children is designed to lead to better tool invention, production, consumption, and handling.

Our body of knowledge and tool development has never given, is not presently giving, and almost surely will never give us either physical security or well-being. The more vast and awesome our tool production has become, the greater our anxiety, hostility, fear, resentment, and aggression. But the direct correlation between our anxiety and tool production is almost beyond our grasp because our intelligence is itself the result of our conditioning by and within that very body of knowledge. Our intelligence is trained to believe that any imperfections in the reality resulting from our activities, such as personal anguish, misery, and fear, simply indicate the need for improvements in the body of knowledge and/or improvements in tool production, distribution, and application. Even as our body of knowledge splits us off from our lives and creates anxiety and unhappiness, it conditions us to believe religiously that escape from our misery lies in perfecting that body of knowledge.

In other words, modern man's difficulties, dangerous beliefs, and feelings of loneliness, spiritual emptiness, and personal weakness are caused by his illusions about, and separation from, the natural world. Well, the Taoists told us this sort of mess would happen. And they told us what we could do about it. Now it's time to see what that is.

THINGS AS THEY ARE

On the 10th of September last, I walked down the
Via Salaria and into the Republic of Utopia, a
quiet country lying eighty years east of Fara Sa-
bina. Noticing the cheerful disposition of the inhabitants, I enquired the cause of their
contentment, and I was told that it was due to
their laws and to the teaching they received from
their earliest school days. . . .

In order to teach small children to observe particulars they practise a kind of game, in which a
number of small objects, e.g., three grains of bar-
ley, a small coin, a blue button . . . are concealed
in the hand. The hand is opened for an instant,
then quickly closed again, and the child is asked
to say what it has seen. For older children the
game is gradually made more elaborate, until finally they all know how their hats and shoes are

made. I was also informed that by learning how to define words these people have succeeded in defining their economic terms, with the result that various iniquities of the stock market and financial world have entirely disappeared from their country, for no one allows himself to be fooled any longer.

These very Taoist words are from *Gold and Work*, by Ezra Pound. But the principle they describe—that of Reality Appreciation—is a great deal older. Before we present some *official* Taoist writings on that sort of thing, we would like to quote from our favorite *un*official Taoist writer, Henry David Thoreau:

Shams and delusions are esteemed for soundest truths, while reality is fabulous. If men would steadily observe realities only, and not allow themselves to be deluded, life, to compare it with such things as we know, would be like a fairy tale and the Arabian Nights' Entertainments. . . . By closing the eyes and slumbering, and consenting to be deceived by shows, men establish and confirm their daily life of routine and habit everywhere, which still is built on purely illusory foundations. Children, who play life, discern its true law and relations more clearly than men, who fail to live it worthily, but who think that they are wiser by experience, that is, by failure. . . . Men esteem truth remote, in the outskirts of the system, behind the farthest star, before Adam and after the last man. In eternity there is indeed something true and sublime. But all these times and places and occasions are now and here. God himself culminates in the present moment, and will never be more divine in the lapse of all the ages. And we are enabled to apprehend at all what is sublime and noble only by the perpetual instilling and drenching of the reality that surrounds us.

Out of the "Hundred Schools" of Chinese philosophy, only two—Confucianism and Taoism—have survived. They have lasted through thousands of years because they have proven the most Useful. The Chinese are very practical people—they have no respect for things that sound good but don't work. In the East generally, and in China especially, philosophy has always been considered of no value unless it can be, and is, applied in one's daily life.

Western philosophy, having little connection with everyday living, is (to this observer, at least) comparatively egocentric and impractical, with much Arguing and Theorizing, and much bounding

back and forth across the intellectual landscape—
a pleasant, part-time diversion formulated by and
aimed at the likes of Owl, Rabbit, and sometimes
Eeyore, but not particularly supportive of the likes
of Piglet and Pooh. Western philosophy has become the domain of pipe-smoking, tweed-suited
college professors (who may profess it but not necessarily practice it) and hypercerebral students
who, for all their intelligence, often seem to have
a hard time washing their clothes or repairing the
lawn mower.

Looking askance at all this, the typical Mind
of the West says: So who needs *Eastern* philosophy? To such a mind, Eastern philosophy has two
things wrong with it. First, it's Eastern—exotic
and mystical, quaint but useless. Second, it's Philosophy. And what good does *that* do anybody?

What this narrow-minded attitude overlooks
is the fact that much of what makes up the Practical West came from the East, and most of that
came from China. And, we might add, a good deal
of it came from the Taoists—China's foremost scientists, inventors, medical men, artists, and observers of the natural world.

In the West we are told in school that Johann
Gutenberg invented movable type, William Har-

vey discovered the circulation of the blood, and
Sir Isaac Newton was the originator of his First
Law of Motion. In reality, these things were invented and discovered in China long before those
men were born. In addition to who-knows-how-
many other things, the Chinese have given the
world the mechanical clock, paper (including wall-
paper, toilet paper, paper handkerchiefs, money,
and playing cards), multicolor printing, porcelain,
lacquer, phosphorescent paint, the magic lantern
(ancestor of the movie projector), the spinning
wheel, the wheelbarrow, the umbrella, the modern plow, harness, seed drill, and rotary win-
nowing fan (as well as the practice of growing crops
in rows), the fishing reel, the modern compass (and
the difference between true and magnetic north),
the seismograph, relief and grid maps, the decimal
system, the calculator, the hermetically sealed research laboratory, the chain drive, the belt drive,
the chain pump, the essentials of the steam en-
gine, dial and pointer devices, cast iron, the manu-
facture of steel from cast iron, the suspension
bridge, the segmental arch (non-semi-circle)
bridge, the contour transport canal, the canal
pound-lock, masts, sails, the rudder, watertight
compartments in ships, the paddle-wheel boat,

land sailing, the kite (including the acrobatic kite, the fighter kite, the message kite, the musical kite, the lighted kite . . .), the hang glider (which, like the acrobatic kite, was developed and flown by Taoist adepts in the mountains of China as a way to learn and work with natural laws), the hot-air balloon, the helicopter rotor, the parachute (fifteen hundred years before Leonardo da Vinci's), tuned bells, "church" (court and temple) bells, equal temperament in music (championed one hundred and thirty-eight years later in the West by Johann Sebastian Bach), drilling for natural gas, the butane gas cylinder (in its original form, a gas-filled bamboo tube with a valve at one end, over which travelers cooked their food on journeys), sunglasses, waterproof clothing, mountain-climbing gear, and gunpowder (which, ironically, was discovered by a Taoist searching for the formula to an elixir of longevity). A group of court ladies invented matches, which were brought to Europe one thousand years later. Some other Chinese discovered the structure of snowflakes—two thousand years ahead of the West—and the existence of sunspots and solar wind. The Chinese discovered diabetes and deficiency diseases and pioneered the sciences of endocrinology, immunology, thyroid hormone therapy, and anatomy (deducing, among other things, the presence and design of the eardrum before its physical discovery). They developed systems of biological pest control . . . Well, that ought to be enough to make the point. These people Noticed things.

Unfortunately, one thing the West did *not* import from the East was the traditional Chinese belief that science, morality, and spirituality must go together; that science without ethical and spiritual considerations was not a whole science, but a form of madness. Oh, well—we can't have everything, we suppose.

Returning to Pooh and friends, this business of scientific observation and so on reminds us of the quite Taoist discovery of the principle of Poohsticks, a game that has been played around the world ever since it was described in *The House at Pooh Corner* (and just *possibly* before). Pooh, as you may remember, had been studying

fir-cones and had made up a rhyme about one in
particular . . .

He had just come to the bridge; and not looking
where he was going, he tripped over something,
and the fir-cone jerked out of his paw into the
river.

"Bother," said Pooh, as it floated slowly under the
bridge, and he went back to get another fir-cone
which had a rhyme to it. But then he thought that
he would just look at the river instead, because it
was a peaceful sort of day, so he lay down and
looked at it, and it slipped slowly away beneath
him . . . and suddenly, there was his fir-cone slipping away too.

"That's funny," said Pooh. "I dropped it on the
other side," said Pooh, "and it came out on this
side! I wonder if it would do it again?" And he
went back for some more fir-cones.

It did. It kept on doing it. Then he dropped two
in at once, and leant over the bridge to see which
of them would come out first; and one of them
did; but as they were both the same size, he didn't
know if it was the one which he wanted to win,
or the other one. So the next time he dropped
one big one and one little one, and the big one

came out first, which was what he had said it would do, and the little one came out last, which was what he had said it would do, so he had won twice . . . and when he went home for tea, he had won thirty-six and lost twenty-eight, which meant that he was—that he had—well, you take twenty-eight from thirty-six, and *that's* what he was. Instead of the other way around.

And that was the beginning of the game called Poohsticks, which Pooh invented, and which he and his friends used to play on the edge of the Forest. But they played with sticks instead of fir-cones, because they were easier to mark.

In that Poohishly humble incident, one can see all the elements of pure science as practiced by the Taoists: the chance occurrence, the observant and inquisitive mind, deduction of the principles involved, application of those principles, modification of materials, and a new practice or way of doing things. Not bad. But after all, Pooh is *That* sort of Bear.

As we have already implied, there is a good deal more to the Importance of Observation than scientific discoveries. There is also the matter of Living Wisely and Well. In this area in particular, we believe, the West could learn a few things from the East. For example, what sort of education in Practical Wisdom do we tend to receive in school?

> There are three hundred cows in a field. The gate has been left open, and two cows pass through it every minute. How many cows are left in the field after an hour and a half?

This sort of thing, we're told, will help us once we graduate—help us apply our learning to everyday matters and, ideally, help us discern the true from the false. But, to return to the terms of the three-hundred-cow math problem: If you have ever herded cattle, you know that cows do not pass through an open gate at the rate of two per minute. They either go through all at once, or not at all. Or they wander through whenever they feel up to it. In all probability, there would be *no* cows left in the field *ten minutes* after a gate was opened, or a fence pulled down. But if you told the teacher that, you would be told that you were wrong. Such is the difference between School and Life. (And if you in school don't believe that such a difference exists, just wait until you get out.)

If we were asked to condense Taoist teachings

regarding everyday life to their irreducible essentials, we would say: Observe, Deduce, and Apply. Watch what is around you—putting aside, as best you can, previous conceptions that you or others might have about it. Ideally, look at it as though you were seeing it for the first time. Mentally reduce it to its basic elements—"See simplicity in complexity," as Lao-tse put it. Use intuition as well as logic in order to understand what you see (a vital difference between the Whole Reasoner and the Left-Brain Technician). Look for connections between one thing and another—notice patterns and relationships. Study the natural laws you see operating through them. Then work with those laws, applying the smallest possible amount of interference and effort, in order to learn more and achieve whatever you need to—and no more.

Once you make a habit of Observing, Deducing, and Applying, you may sense a pathway opening up ahead of you—or inside of you, or both—leading to a deeper understanding of things. You may even feel at times as though you're in some sort of Other Dimension, like Thoreau's example of the Arabian Nights' Entertainments. But you're not, really; you're just seeing and experiencing Things As They Are, rather than as someone-or-other *says* they are. And the difference between the two can be considerable.

In a sense, though, the image of another dimension is an appropriate one. For as you follow the Way, you leave the land of Either/Or and enter the land of Both. As Lao-tse wrote in the first chapter of the *Tao Te Ching*, many people are unable to follow the Way because they are unable to *see* it, being stuck in Either/Or:

> *Those habitually without desires*
> *Perceive [the Way] as "subtlety."*
> *Those habitually with desires*
> *Perceive it as "action."*
> *These two have the same source,*
> *But different names.*
> *Together they're called "darkness"—*
> *Darkness of increasing darkness,*
> *All mystery's gateway.*

In other words, Tao is both "subtlety" *and* "action." Those who consider it only as spirit and ignore its forms, or who notice its forms but disregard what is behind and within them, know of only half of it, at best—neither the Spiritual people who deny the world nor the Physical people who deny the spirit can know of and follow the Way. But *you* can.

"I feel dizzy," said Piglet, who had been reading over my shoulder.

"Yes, I did get a bit carried away, didn't I?"

"Isn't there some other way of explaining all that?"

"I suppose. Let's try it like this . . ."

Taoism is not the reject-the-physical-world way of living that some scholars (and a few Taoists) would have others believe. Even Lao-tse, the most reclusive of Taoist writers, wrote, "Honor all under heaven as your body." To a Taoist, a reject-the-physical-world approach would be an extremist absurdity, impossible to live—without dying. Instead, a Taoist might say: Carefully observe the natural laws in operation in the world around you, and live by them. From following them, you will learn the morality of modesty, moderation, compassion, and consideration (not just one society's rules and regulations), the wisdom of seeing things as they are (not of merely collecting "facts" about them), and the happiness of being in harmony with the Way (which has nothing to do with self-

righteous "spiritual" obsessions and fanaticism).
And you will live lightly, spontaneously, and
effortlessly.

"Well, Piglet?"

"Could you tell some stories?"

"Yes, I suppose I could."

"Stories?" said Pooh, opening his eyes.

"I *would* like to hear some stories," said
Piglet.

"So would I," said Pooh. "All seriousness
aside."

"All . . . Yes. All seriousness aside. Let's
see—we were just mentioning observation, spontaneity, and effortlessness . . . Would you like to
hear 'The Old Master and the Horse'?"

"We won't know," said Pooh, "until we've
heard it."

"True enough. This is how it goes . . ."

A horse was tied outside a shop in a narrow Chinese village street. Whenever anyone would try
to walk by, the horse would kick him. Before long,
a small crowd of villagers had gathered near the
shop, arguing about how best to get past the dan-

gerous horse. Suddenly, someone came running. "The Old Master is coming!" he shouted. "*He'll* know what to do!"

The crowd watched eagerly as the Old Master came around the corner, saw the horse, turned, and walked down another street.

"You see," I said, "the Old Master lived the principle of *Wu Wei*, or Effortless Action. That's something the Taoists say we can learn by watching water."

"Water?" asked Piglet.

"When a stream comes to some stones in its path, it doesn't struggle to remove them, or fight against them, or *think* about them. It just goes around them. And as it does, it sings. Water responds to What's There with effortless action."

"I think I missed something," said Pooh.

"Missed something where?" I asked.

"In the story—"

"Oh, that. The Old Master knew he didn't have to go down that street. He knew he could go another way."

"But why didn't the others know?"

"Ah! Precisely. Why *didn't* they know?"

"*I* wouldn't have gone down that street,"
squeaked Piglet. "Not with a horse in the way. Or
a goat. Or a dog. Or anything."

"But why didn't the others—"

"My dear Pooh," said Owl, flying over to the
writing table. "In problems of this sort, one must
consider the Physical Properties involved."

"I didn't know there were any," replied Pooh,
rubbing his ear.

"*That is to say,*" continued Owl, somewhat
annoyed, "the street in question was narrow, the
horse was large—and furthermore it was Belligerent."

"Further along it was what?"

"It kicked. The Old Master knew that it was
Futile to Proceed—"

"We know that, Owl," I said. "The point is—"

Oh, well—so much for stories. Let's go on to
the next principle.

When you observe the natural world, you'll
eventually see that everything in it is designed to
succeed—including what some might judge to be
"bad." If you want to learn the natural world's
principles of success, you'll need to see things not
as "good" or "bad," but as they are. This does

not mean discard morality, or common sense, or anything of the sort; it simply means—well, let's show what it means by a couple of examples.

Many centuries ago, the Chinese empress Si Ling-chi overheard complaints that "worms," or moth larvae, were devouring the leaves of the royal mulberry tree. So she went out to see what was happening. She watched the larvae as they spun their cocoons of strong, shimmering threads. Observing their movements as they spun, she conceived of a way to extract the fibers and weave clothing material from them. Her observations and experiments led to the cultivation of what was to become the most highly treasured of all the world's natural fibers—the magical material known as silk.

On returning from a walk about forty years ago, the Swiss engineer George deMestral found cockleburs clinging to his clothing. Unlike countless other people who have cursed the prickly seedpods, picked them off, and discarded them, he asked himself, "Why do they stick?" Examining them closely, he found that they were covered with tiny hooks, which had become embedded in the loops of his clothing fabric. He wondered if it would be possible to develop fasteners based on a hook-and-loop principle, which would by their nature be more flexible than anything then being used. From his watching and wondering came Velcro—from "velvet crochet," or "velvet hook"—fastening systems made from which are now used all over the world, in applications too numerous to mention.

Despite the tired old claim that Necessity is the Mother of Invention, it's usually Observation and Imagination that deserve the credit. The major portion of useful inventions, knowledge, and achievement has been brought about by curious, childlike, creative observers of the world around them, whose vision is unclouded by judgments of what is "possible" or "impossible," "good" or "bad." The telescope, for example, was invented in principle by some Dutch children playing with defective lenses discarded from the shop of a spectacles maker. They found that when the lenses were held one in front of another—which, of course, *everyone* knew was not supposed to be done—distant objects appeared closer. News of their discovery spread to Italy and to the eager attention of a man named Galileo Galilei . . .

When you see beyond "good" and "bad," you are much better able to recognize and make the most of What's There. For example, when a

Bear overeats a bit and gets stuck in your front door . . .

. . . you can use his legs to hang the washing on. And then use the *back* door.

"That's Owl in the next room, isn't it?" I asked. "What's he talking about now?"

"He wants to apply for a job as a radio announcer," said Piglet. "He's practicing on Rabbit."

"Oh? Let's go in and see what he has to say. This should be interesting."

"Ladies and Gentlemen," Owl was proclaiming. "For a truly Malicious treat—"

"That's *de*licious," corrected Rabbit.

"Hello, Owl," I said. "Just what product are you trying to sell, anyway?"

"*Professor Padbury's Shredded Oak,*" Owl replied.

"Oh. Professor . . . I beg your pardon—did you say *Oats*, or *Oak*?"

"Oak."

"I see. In that case, you had it right the first time. Malicious."

"And look here, Owl—do you really want to get involved in this business? Promoting products that don't necessarily do anybody any good, making wild claims, and all that?"

"I thought," said Owl, "that with my voice—"

"Yes, your melodious voice. But surely you could do something better with it. This may be no affair of mine, but if I could show you the true nature of advertising . . . I know—let me play you a recording I made when I was an investigative reporter. Ah, here it is. Now, listen to this—I'm interviewing Rasmussen Slick, chairman of the American Tobacco Advertising Council . . ."

"Mr. Slick, many people have pointed out that tobacco advertising today hardly ever shows anyone smoking a cigarette—nor does it show ashtrays, smoke, tobacco ash, and other things people would naturally associate with your product. I'm sure you wouldn't want to show cancer wards and lung operations . . . But aren't those illustrations of clear mountain streams, snowy hillsides, healthy skiers, and so on just a *little* evasive and misleading? What could you say about that?"

"Well, first of all, young man, the American public for many, many years now has been deluged with statements alleging that tobacco is directly responsible for health problems of various kinds. I would like to say that the proof behind such assertions is entirely lacking. What we are attempting to do is merely provide a reasonable counterbalance to such ridiculous claims, and show our product in a better, fairer light. I am proud to say that I have been a cigarette smoker myself for

many years now, and I have *never* (cough) suffered
in any way because of my habit, which I find pleasant, soothing, and (ahem) relaxing. (*A*hem.) Nothing, I repeat *nothing* (cough, cough) could be
further from the truth (wheeze) than to (COUGH)
claim, as so many now are (HACK, HACK, HACK)—
say, couldn't we shut that thing off for a while?"

"Well, Owl?"

"Perhaps," said Owl thoughtfully, "I ought to
apply for a teaching position at the University."

Perhaps. And then again, perhaps not. We're
not so sure that Owl would prove a vital addition
to the faculty. For one unfortunate thing about
Owl—now that he has so thoughtfully inserted
himself into this chapter to provide an example
of it—is that he has an Image to maintain. And
Maintaining an Image tends to get in the way of
seeing What's There. If one can't clearly see
What's There, how can one *learn* it? And if one
can't learn it, how can one *teach* it?

You may recall what happened when Rabbit
found a notice from Christopher Robin saying
"GON OUT BACKSON BISY BACKSON," and
took it to Owl for his Wise Counsel . . .

Owl took Christopher Robin's notice from Rabbit and looked at it nervously. He could spell his own name WOL, and he could spell Tuesday so that you knew it wasn't Wednesday, and he could read quite comfortably when you weren't looking over his shoulder and saying "Well?" all the time, and he could—

"Well?" said Rabbit.

"Yes," said Owl, looking Wise and Thoughtful. "I see what you mean. Undoubtedly."

"Well?"

"Exactly," said Owl. "Precisely." And he added, after a little thought, "If you had not come to me, I should have come to you."

"Why?" asked Rabbit.

"For that very reason," said Owl, hoping that something helpful would happen soon.

"Yesterday morning," said Rabbit solemnly, "I went to see Christopher Robin. He was out. Pinned on his door was a notice."

"The same notice?"

"A different one. But the meaning was the same. It's very odd."

"Amazing," said Owl, looking at the notice again, and getting, just for a moment, a curious sort of feeling that something had happened to Christopher Robin's back. "What did you do?"

"Nothing."

"The best thing," said Owl wisely.

"Well?" said Rabbit again, as Owl knew he was going to.

"Exactly," said Owl.

For a little while he couldn't think of anything more; and then, all of a sudden, he had an idea.

"Tell me, Rabbit," he said, "the *exact* words of the first notice. This is very important. Everything depends on this. The *exact* words of the *first* notice."

"It was just the same as that one really."

Owl looked at him, and wondered whether to push him off the tree; but, feeling that he could always do it afterwards, he tried once more to find out what they were talking about.

"The exact words, please," he said, as if Rabbit hadn't spoken.

"It just said, 'Gon out. Backson.' Same as this, only this says 'Bisy Backson' too."

Owl gave a great sigh of relief.

"Ah!" said Owl. "*Now* we know where we are."

"Yes, but where's Christopher Robin?" said Rabbit. "That's the point."

Owl looked at the notice again. To one of his education the reading of it was easy. "Gone out, Backson. Bisy, Backson"—just the sort of thing you'd expect to see on a notice.

"It is quite clear what has happened, my dear Rabbit," he said. "Christopher Robin has gone out somewhere with Backson. He and Backson are busy together. Have you seen a Backson anywhere about in the Forest lately?"

As it turned out, Rabbit wasn't any better than Owl at determining the meaning of the notice, because he too has an Image to maintain—an image of Captain-Rabbit-in-charge-of-the-situation, which involves so much rushing about, so much excitement and what-in-the-world, that it leaves him little time to sit down and reflect on what something is.

"Hallo, Pooh," said Rabbit.

"Hallo, Rabbit," said Pooh dreamily.

"Did you make that song up?"

"Well, I sort of made it up," said Pooh. "It isn't Brain," he went on humbly, "because You Know Why, Rabbit; but it comes to me sometimes."

"Ah!" said Rabbit, who never let things come to him, but always went and fetched them. "Well, the point is, have you seen a Spotted or Herbaceous Backson in the Forest, at all?"

"No," said Pooh. "Not a—no," said Pooh. "I saw Tigger just now."

"That's no good."

"No," said Pooh. "I thought it wasn't."

"Have you seen Piglet?"

"Yes," said Pooh. "I suppose *that* isn't any good either?" he asked meekly.

"Well, it depends if he saw anything."

"He saw me," said Pooh.

Rabbit sat down on the ground next to Pooh and, feeling much less important like that, stood up again.

One of the many advantages of seeing Things As They Are is that we can solve problems through observation and deduction. After all, how can we solve problems if we can't first clearly see what they are? And the best time to see them is in the beginning. Most major difficulties are caused by a failure to observe the minor difficulties that they start out as. "Trouble is easily stopped before it commences," wrote Lao-tse. "Put things in order before chaos occurs." In other words, an ounce of prevention is worth a pound of pesticide. The overwhelming tendency in unobservant industrial society, however, is to ignore small problems until they become enormous—and then panic.

"Call out the troops! Mad Tyrant Number Twelve is taking over the world! We've got to stop him—even if we have to kill half a million people doing it! Oh, it's simply awful!" Well, let's see . . . Who sold him his weaponry? We did. Who trained his military forces in the use of it? We did. Who supplied the materials he wanted? We did. Who supported his vicious dictatorship for years because he persecuted our "enemies"? We did. And who ignored his unstable personality, his destruction of anyone who opposed him, and his repeated threats against world order for all that time? We did. So there you are.

What can be just as hard to see as problems-in-the-making is that a good many "problems" aren't really problems to begin with. People who don't see situations for what they are often struggle against difficulties that aren't there and *create* difficulties in the process. Or turn small difficulties into large ones. Compounding any problem (or nonproblem) is the traditional Western response to difficulties real or imagined: the tendency to see them *emotionally*, perceiving them as threats to one's personal survival—threats that must be fought tooth-and-nail to the bitter end. In the East, such an approach to life is considered rather immature. Overdoing it, you know; wasting energy. Or, as the Chinese saying puts it, "Painting legs on the snake."

So in solving problems, one needs to know if they *are* problems. Is what appears at first to be bad *truly* bad? The following selected Taoist writings show the importance of that question. The first is our streamlined version of a story by Liu An, also known as Huai-nan-tse:

> An old man and his son lived in an abandoned fortress on the side of a hill. Their only possession of value was a horse.

One day, the horse ran away. The neighbors came by to offer sympathy. "That's really bad!" they said. "How do you know?" asked the old man.

The next day, the horse returned, bringing with it several wild horses. The old man and his son shut them all inside the gate. The neighbors hurried over. "That's really good!" they said. "How do you know?" asked the old man.

The following day, the son tried riding one of the wild horses, fell off, and broke his leg. The neighbors came around as soon as they heard the news. "That's really bad!" they said. "How do you know?" asked the old man.

The day after that, the army came through, forcing the local young men into service to fight a faraway battle against the northern barbarians. Many of them would never return. But the son couldn't go, because he'd broken his leg.

The second selection is by Chuang-tse:

Once when Duke Huan was passing by a marsh, a goblin appeared in the road before him. The duke turned to Kuan Chung, who was driving the carriage. "Do you see anything in the road ahead of us?" he asked. "I see nothing," Kuan Chung replied.

By the time the duke returned home, he was speaking incoherently, and had become ill. For several days, he remained in his bed.

An officer named Huang Kao-ao called on the duke. "How could a goblin harm you?" he asked. "You are injuring yourself. If your vital energy is weakened by fears and anxieties, you will become seriously ill."

"But do goblins exist?" asked the duke.

"Yes, they do. By small mountain lakes, you will find the *Li*; around fires, the *Ch'ieh*; in the dust, the *Lei-t'ing*. In low-lying areas of the northeast are the *Pei-a* and the *Wa-lung*. In the north-western lowlands can be found the *I-Yang*. The *Wang-hsiang* live near rivers, the *Hsin* in the hills, the *K'uei* in the mountains, and the *Fang-huang* in wild places. Around marshes can be found the *Wei-t'o*."

"Describe the *Wei-t'o*," said the duke.

"A *Wei-t'o* is as big around as the hub of a carriage wheel, and as tall as the length of an axle. It wears a purple robe and red cap. It hates the sound of passing vehicles, and when it hears one, it claps its hands over its ears. Whoever sees a *Wei-t'o* is destined to become a great ruler."

"That is what I saw!" exclaimed the duke. He sat up and straightened his clothes. He began to laugh. By the end of the day, his illness had vanished.

The third selection also is by Chuang-tse, who uses an event in the difficult life of K'ung Fu-tse to illustrate a Taoist attitude:

The armies of Ch'en and Ts'ai were locked in battle, and K'ung Fu-tse was caught between them. For seven days, he had had nothing to eat but coarse soup. Although much tiredness showed on his face, he spent the time singing and playing his lute.

Outside the house in which he was staying, two disciples discussed the situation. "Twice now the Master has been driven from Lu. He had to run from Wei. In Sung, the very tree beneath which he rested was cut down. In both Shang and Chou, he was faced with the most extreme difficulties. Now here he is between Ch'en and Ts'ai. He could easily be killed or taken prisoner. Yet he plays his lute and sings! What irresponsible behavior!"

Their words were repeated to K'ung Fu-tse, who pushed aside his lute and remarked, "They speak like small men. Call them in, and I will talk to them."

The two disciples entered the room. "Master," said one, "we are concerned about your conduct. It seems very strange, considering that you are presently in great distress."

"Oh, am I?" K'ung Fu-tse replied. "When a man operates in harmony with the Way of Heaven, his teachings cannot help but succeed. When he cuts himself off from the Way of Heaven, his teachings cannot help but fail. Looking within and examining myself, I see that I am acting in harmony with the Way of Heaven. I have the principles with which to overcome the terrible disintegration that I see around me. Yet you say that I am in distress! There may be difficulty at the moment, but I will not lose the Virtue that I possess. It is when the ice and snow are on them that we see the strength of the cypress and the pine. I am grateful for this trouble around me, because it gives me an opportunity to realize how fortunate I am." He turned back to his lute, and played again.

The first disciple began to dance. "I did not realize before how high and deep are the ways of heaven and earth!" the second one exclaimed.

Is "good" necessarily good? Is "bad" necessarily bad? It's considered good to be beautiful, but many people through being beautiful have ruined their lives and the lives of others. It's considered bad to be unattractive, but because of being unattractive, many have come to concern themselves with matters more important than surface appearance and have gone on to make something Special of themselves—in quite a few cases becoming Beautiful in the process. It's considered good to be healthy and strong, but many energetic people lose their health and strength by taking what they have for granted, not knowing what it's like to be old and depleted—and therefore not taking care of themselves—until it's Too Late. It's considered bad to be ill and weak, but many have responded to such conditions by examining their lives and changing their ways of doing things, thereby building up their health and strength to remarkable degrees. Unattractiveness, illness, and weakness have many valuable lessons to teach to those willing to learn from them.

It's considered good to live a long life, but many spend their long lives sitting and complaining, watching television, describing their operations, and retelling for the umpteenth time what Aunt Gertrude said forty years ago. Many Great

Achievers died young, yet lived every minute of the time they had. As Chuang-tse pointed out, even death itself may not necessarily be bad:

How do we know that to cling to life is not an error? Perhaps our fear of its end approaching is like forgetting our way and not knowing how to return home.

Li Chi was a daughter of the border chieftain Ai Feng. When Duke Hsien claimed her as his wife, she cried until her sleeves were soaked with tears. But after she had come to know the duke and had shared his palace, she laughed at her former fears and sadness. How do we know that the spirits of the dead do not do the same?

Those who dream of feasting may awaken to hunger and sorrow. Those who dream of hunger may, when they awaken, rise and join a hunting party. While they were asleep, they did not realize that they were dreaming. . . . But when they awoke, they knew. Someday will come a great awakening, when we will know this life was like a dream. . . .

These words may seem strange, but many years from now we might meet someone who can explain them, unexpectedly some morning or evening.

In the meantime, we can look clearly at our lives and the life around us, and Live. Before we start crying and praying to the Universe to take away our Trials and Tribulations, we might more closely examine what it has given us. Maybe the "good" things are tests, possibly rather difficult ones at that, and the "bad" things are gifts to help us grow: problems to solve, situations to learn to avoid, habits to change, conditions to accept, lessons to learn, things to transform—all opportunities to find Wisdom, Happiness, and Truth. To quote William Blake:

> *It is right it should be so;*
> *Man was made for Joy and Woe;*
> *And when this we rightly know,*
> *Thro' the World we safely go.*
> *Joy and Woe are woven fine,*
> *A Clothing for the soul divine.*

Hmm. Everyone seems to have left.

"*I'm* still here," said Piglet.
"Oh—so you are."
"I enjoyed the stories."
"That's good."

"They helped me to . . . *reflect* on things."

"Things?" Such as—"

"*Fear*."

"Oh."

"Well, I'm going out on a walk, to do some thinking. I'll be back in a bit."

"Right you are. Have a pleasant time."

When we see Things As They Are, we find a world of Magic—the world that has been there all along. And we find ourselves wondering how we ever missed it. As Henry David Thoreau wrote:

> What is a course of history or philosophy, or poetry, no matter how well selected, or the best society, or the most admirable routine of life, compared with the discipline of looking always at what is to be seen? Will you be a reader, a student merely, or a seer? Read your fate, see what is before you, and walk on into futurity.

And now, here's a Riddle for Piglet, when he returns: If "good" is not necessarily good, and "bad" not necessarily bad, what is "small"?

THE UPRIGHT HEART

The wind was against them now, and Piglet's ears streamed behind him like banners as he fought his way along, and it seemed hours before he got them into the shelter of the Hundred Acre Wood and they stood up straight again, to listen, a little nervously, to the roaring of the gale among the treetops.

"Supposing a tree fell down, Pooh, when we were underneath it?"

"Supposing it didn't," said Pooh after careful thought.

Piglet was comforted by this, and in a little while they were knocking and ringing very cheerfully at Owl's door.

And now it's time for—what's that squeaking noise?

There's not much you can do
When you're only Very Small . . .
The Great Deeds aren't for you.
They're important
As they can be,
But you can't do those things at all.

"*Piglet*? Whatever in the world—"

"Pooh's been giving me songing lessons," squeaked Piglet.

"Don't you mean *singing* les— oh, well, no, I guess that's right. Songing lessons. Oh, he has, has he?"

"Yes."

"Well, I only hope he realizes what he's unleashed upon an unsuspecting world."

"Hello," said Pooh. "Has Piglet sung you his song?"

"Some of it, at least. He sings awfully high, doesn't he? In the human world, he'd be known as a Countertenor."

"No," said Pooh. "He can count higher than that."

"Higher than what?"

"Ten."

"Who said anything about counting, Pooh?"

"You *said* that Piglet is a count-to-tenner. And *I* said—"

"Yes, yes. What I meant was, he sings high."

"After all," said Pooh, "he's a Very Small Animal."

"Indeed," added Piglet. "You can't expect a pig to sing like *Pooh*. He's a Bearitone."

"Piglet, what an awful joke."

"Joke?" said Pooh. "Where?"

What was I about to say? Oh, yes. Now we come to the power of the Sensitive, the Modest, and the Small—a power that all Piglets have in potential, whether or not they do anything with it. Of all the teachings of East or West, Taoism places the greatest emphasis on that power, which in Taoist writings is personified in its varying aspects as the Child, the Mysterious Female, and the Spirit of the Valley. Significantly, these are also personifications of the Tao itself.

Let's begin our examination of the Sensitive, the Modest, and the Small by considering Sensitivity. In the West, sensitivity is considered a Minus rather than a Plus. ("Oh, you're just too *sensitive!*") But even in denouncing it as something to get rid of, the West acknowledges a little of its tremendous power. For example, it is widely recognized that being negatively sensitive about one's health through worry-imagery and pessimistic self-talk can make and keep one sick. What is not so widely recognized, however, is that being *positively* sensitive about one's health—"listening" to the body, avoiding damaging influences, imagining and directing healing energy, visualizing perfect health, and so on—can make and keep one well, as an increasing number of people are discovering, some of them through curing themselves of "incurable" illnesses.

Sensitivity and skill develop together—as one of them increases in the process of learning something, so does the other. A skilled ballet dancer is aware of his muscles as they stretch and contract, tighten and relax, through exercise, practice, and performance. Applying that sensitivity, he leaps, twirls and lands without apparent effort. A skilled athlete of any sort is aware of just how to move, how to hit or throw a ball in the right way at the right time, how to do this or that in order to score a point. Our last *T'ai Chi Ch'üan* teacher had developed his awareness to such an extent that he would immediately know when anyone was trying to sneak up behind him. In their areas, at least,

the masters of any such skills are very sensitive—
and therefore very alert. As Chuang-tse wrote:

> Those of perfect Virtue cannot be burned by fire,
> nor drowned by water. Neither can they be
> harmed by heat or cold, nor injured by wild ani-
> mals. It is not that they are indifferent—it is that
> they discriminate between where they may safely
> rest and where they will be in danger. Watchful
> in prosperity and adversity, cautious in their com-
> ings and goings, nothing can injure them.

Nothing, that is, as long as they avoid having
tea in a storm up in a tree at Owl's house . . .

There was a loud cracking noise.

"Look out!" cried Pooh. "Mind the clock! Out of
the way, Piglet! Piglet, I'm falling on you!"

"Help!" cried Piglet.

Pooh's side of the room was slowly tilting upwards
and his chair began sliding down on Piglet's. The
clock slithered gently along the mantlepiece, collecting vases on the way, until they all crashed
together on to what had once been the floor, but
was now trying to see what it looked like as a wall.
[The portrait of] Uncle Robert, who was going to

be the new hearthrug, and was bringing the rest of his wall with him as carpet, met Piglet's chair just as Piglet was expecting to leave it, and for a little while it became very difficult to remember which was really the north. Then there was another loud crack . . . Owl's room collected itself feverishly . . . and there was silence.

Well—so Owl's house in the trees is now on Ground Level. *That's* a fine piece of cake.

"Cake?" said Pooh.

The word for Taoist sensitivity is Cooperate. As Lao-tse wrote, "The skilled walker leaves no tracks"—he is sensitive to (and therefore respectful toward) his surroundings and works with the natural laws that govern them. Like a chameleon, he blends in with What's There. And he does this through the awareness that comes from reducing the Ego to nothing. As Chuang-tse put it:

To him who dwells not in himself, the forms of things reveal themselves as they are. He moves like water, reflects like a mirror, responds like an echo. His lightness makes him seem to disappear. Still as a clear lake, he is harmonious in his relations with those around him, and remains so through profit and loss. He does not precede others, but follows them instead.

"But where's the cake?" asked Pooh.

"Please, Pooh—I'm in the middle of this. Go look in the refrigerator."

"There's nothing in the refrigerator."

"Oh? Well, don't blame *me*."

The Taoist alchemist and herbalist Ko Hung described one of the benefits of nonegotistical awareness: contentment.

The contented man can be happy with what appears to be useless. He can find worthwhile occupation in forests and mountains. He stays in a small cottage and associates with the simple. He would not exchange his worn clothes for the imperial robes, nor the load on his back for a four-horse carriage. He leaves the jade in the mountain and the pearls in the sea. Wherever he goes, whatever he does, he can be happy—he knows when to stop. He does not pick the brief-blossoming flower; he does not travel the dangerous road. To him, the ten thousand possessions are dust in the wind. He sings as he travels among the green mountains.

He finds sheltering branches more comforting than red-gated mansions, the plow in his hands more rewarding than the prestige of titles and banners, fresh mountain water more satisfying than the feasts of the wealthy. He acts in true freedom. What can competition for honors mean to him? What attraction can anxiety and greed possibly hold? Through simplicity he has Tao, and from Tao, everything. He sees the light in the "darkness," the clear in the "cloudy," the speed in the "slowness," the full in the "empty." The cook creating a meal with his own hands has as much honor in his eyes as a famous singer or high official. He has no profits to gain, no salary to lose; no applause, no criticism. When he looks up, it is not in envy. When he looks down, it is not with arrogance. Many look at him, but nobody sees him. Calm and detached, he is free from all danger, a dragon hidden among men.

Hidden. That reminds us of What's-his-name.

In a corner of the room, the table-cloth began to wriggle. Then it wrapped itself into a ball and rolled across the room.

Then it jumped up and down once or twice, and put out two ears.

It rolled across the room again, and unwound itself.

With the reappearance of Piglet, we come to the second admired characteristic we mentioned at the beginning of the chapter: Modesty. Which brings us to one of our favorite selections from the writings of Chuang-tse:

On a trip to Sung, Yang-tse spent the night at an inn. The innkeeper had two wives, one beautiful, the other very plain. The plain one was treated with honor and affection, but the beautiful one was ignored. The next day, Yang-tse asked a boy of the household why. He replied, "The beautiful one knows that she is beautiful; the plain one knows that she is plain."

When Yang-tse returned, he addressed his disciples: "Remember this, my followers. Put away your pride, and act upon your Virtue. If you do this, how can you not be loved?"

As that story so perfectly sums up the subject of Modesty, we think, let's go on to that of the Small.

"Have you anything to say about the Small, Piglet?"

"Why, yes," he replied. "I was just rehearsing it (ahem)."

There's not much you can be
When you're not so very tall,
And the Life you long for
Is so high up
You can't reach it—
You're a Very Small Animal.

What if I could be Bigger, and
What if I could be Tall?
Think what I could accomplish then.
As it is, I'm too small,
Much too small.

"Thank you, Piglet. That's about what I thought you'd say."

To the typical mind of the West, Bigger is Better: The large man is a better fighter than the little man, the huge corporation is superior to the small company, the adult is wiser than the child. The Taoist attitude is: Not so.

Is the large man a better fighter than the little man? Our previously mentioned *T'ai Chi Ch'üan* teacher, a small man even by Chinese standards, was once trapped in a Hong Kong alley by a gang of armed thugs. They lost. In martial arts, as in Real Life, it's not the *big* opponent one needs to watch out for; it's the *little* one. There are many reasons, some physical (lower center of gravity), some mental (tricks learned from being the Underdog), some emotional (without interference from a Muscleman Ego, one can move very fast). Large men tend to be lazy and slow, relying on their muscles to carry them through a situation. Little men tend to be far more energetic, flexible, and alert, with finer-tuned nervous systems and less weight to haul around. We've so often seen small fighters dance around their larger opponents, strike them at will and dance out of range, that we laugh when we're told what a Big Bruiser so-and-so is. What does it matter if he's as big as a boxcar, if he can't catch you? To illustrate what we mean, here's the Chinese story of "The Monkeys and the Grasshoppers":

One day a long time ago, some monkeys who lived on a mountain decided they would rather live in the valley below, where it was warmer. But when they went down to the valley, they were bothered by grasshoppers. So they tried to persuade the grasshoppers to leave, first by coaxing and then by threats. But the grasshoppers refused to go. "You puny creatures!" roared the Head Monkey. "If you won't leave, we'll force you out! Tomorrow we'll fight you to the finish!" "All right," said the Head Grasshopper. "If that's the way you want it."

The next day the monkeys marched into the valley, armed with heavy clubs. "Come out, grasshoppers!" they called. "Where are you?" "Here we are!" answered the grasshoppers, as they leaped onto their opponents. *Whack, whack, whack* went the clubs, as one monkey battered another. The grasshoppers were too fast for them. The Head Monkey found to his disgust that the Head Grasshopper had landed on his nose. "I'll get him, boss!" said the monkey next to him. He struck a ferocious blow with his club, missing the grasshopper (who by then had leaped away) but squashing the Head Monkey's nose deep between his eyes. And so it went with one monkey's nose after another. Finally the monkeys staggered away, and the valley was peaceful once again.

And that is why monkeys avoid the valleys, and why they have squashed noses.

For the second point: *Is* the huge corporation superior to the small company? That sort of Dinosaur Mentality didn't work very well for the dinosaurs in the long run, and it doesn't seem to be working very well for businesses, either, as time goes by.

As we are told in school, the dinosaurs were the most successful creatures on earth—for a while. But geographic and climatic changes eliminated them because they couldn't Adapt, and couldn't compete with the smaller, faster creatures that superceded them. Their most plentiful descendants alive today, scientists tell us, are birds—small, adaptable, and mobile.

For some time now, big companies have been buying smaller companies, only to be bought in turn by giant corporations, which are then bought by multinational conglomerates. The bigger they grow, and the more interdependent they make themselves in the process, the more vulnerable they become. Bigness easily becomes its own worst enemy. As recent events continue to show, it doesn't take all that much to put a large corporation in trouble. And the bigger it is, the harder it will fall. Survival of the Fattest may have been the rule of business prosperity for a while. But it's now being supplanted by the Success of the Small. In search of something new and useful, creative businessmen have begun to study the fighting tactics of the Samurai. They might do better, we think, to read the *Tao Te Ching*: "The hard and mighty shall fall; the flexible and yielding shall survive." Just a thought.

There was a disturbance behind the table in the other corner of the room, and Owl was with them again.

"Ah, Piglet," said Owl, looking very much annoyed; "where's Pooh?"

"I'm not quite sure," said Pooh.

For the final point on Bigger is Better: *Is* the adult wiser than the child? On the individual level, of course, the answer depends on which adult and which child. But beyond that, wisdom is to the Taoist a child's state. Children are born with it; most adults have lost it, or a good deal of it. And those who haven't are, in one way or another, like children. Is it a Mere Coincidence that the Chinese suffix *tse*, which has come to mean "master," literally means *child*? As the Confucianist-yet-surprisingly-Taoist philosopher Meng-tse wrote,

"Great man retains child's mind." And, as the following story by Chuang-tse shows, the great man *respects* the child's mind, as well:

Accompanied by six of his wisest men, the Yellow Emperor journeyed to Chu-T'zu Mountain, to speak to the mystic Ta Kuei. In the wilderness of Hsiang Ch'eng, the procession lost its way. After wandering for some time, the men came upon a boy tending horses. "Do you know the way to Chu T'zu Mountain?" they asked him. "I do," the boy replied. "In that case," they said, "would you know where we might find the hidden dwelling of the hermit Ta Kuei?" "Yes," he answered, "I can tell you." "What a fascinating child!" said the emperor to his companions. "He knows this much . . . Let me test him." He stepped from his carriage, and called the boy to him.

"Tell me," said the Yellow Emperor. "If you were in charge of the empire, how would you go about ruling it?"

"I know only the tending of horses," the boy replied. "Is ruling the empire any different from that?"

Not satisfied, the emperor questioned him again:

"I realize that governing is hardly your concern.

Still, I would like to know if you have ever had any thoughts about it."

The boy did not answer. The emperor asked him once more. The boy replied by asking, "Is governing the empire different from tending horses?"

"Explain the tending of horses," said the Yellow Emperor, "and I will tell you."

"When taking care of horses," said the boy, "we make sure that no harm comes to them. In doing so, we put aside anything within ourselves that would injure them. Can ruling a nation differ from that?"

The Yellow Emperor bowed his head twice to the ground. "Heavenly Master!" he exclaimed.

"Does it have pink icing?" asked Pooh.
"Pooh, whatever are you talking about?"
"The *cake*."
"*What* cake?"
"The cake you mentioned. 'A fine piece of cake,' you said."
"Oh, that. That was just an expression."
"Oh."
"Pooh, don't you ever think of anything but your stomach?"

"I hardly ever think about my stomach," said Pooh.

"Well—I'm glad to hear that."

"Mostly, I think about food."

"Well!" said Owl. "This is a nice state of things!"

"What are we going to do, Pooh? Can you think of anything?" asked Piglet.

"Well, I *had* just thought of something," said Pooh. "It was just a little thing I thought of." And he began to sing:

I lay on my chest
And I thought it best
To pretend I was having an evening rest;
I lay on my tum
And I tried to hum
But nothing particular seemed to come.
My face was flat
On the floor, and that
Is all very well for an acrobat;
But it doesn't seem fair
To a Friendly Bear
To stiffen him out with a basket-chair.
And a sort of sqoze

Which grows and grows
Is not too nice for his poor old nose,
And a sort of squch
Is much too much
For his neck and his mouth
   and his ears and such.

"That was all," said Pooh.

Owl coughed in an unadmiring sort of way, and said that, if Pooh was sure that *was* all, they could now give their minds to the Problem of Escape.

"Because," said Owl, "we can't go out by what used to be the front door. Something's fallen on it."

Returning to Taoist principles for a moment: When we eliminate interference from the Ego, the energy of the Universal Way can flow through us unimpeded. Which is one reason why Taoists emphasize the importance of being Small, as does Lao-tse in the twenty-eighth chapter of the *Tao Te Ching*:

Know the masculine,
But keep to the feminine.

Become a river
To all under heaven.
As a river flows,
Move in constant Virtue;
Return to the infant state.

Know the light,
But keep to the shadow.
Become a pattern
To all under heaven.
As a pattern repeats itself,
Act in constant Virtue;
Return to the beginning.

Know the high,
But keep to the low.
Become a valley
To all under heaven.
As a valley provides in abundance,
Give in constant Virtue;
Return to natural simplicity.

When we work with the Power of the Small, we follow the example of the Way itself, as Lao-tse pointed out in chapter thirty-four:

The Great Way flows everywhere,
To the left and to the right.
The ten thousand things

Depend on it for life.
It nourishes them all,
Holding nothing back.
It accomplishes what needs to be,
But takes no credit.
It clothes and feeds all things,
Yet does not claim
To be their lord.
It asks for nothing in return.
It may be called the Small.

The ten thousand things
Follow it,
Return to it.
Yet it does not claim
To be their lord.
Therefore, it may be called
The Great.

So too the wise may become great,
By becoming small.

Meanwhile, back at Owl's house . . .

"But how else *can* you get out?" asked Piglet anxiously.

"That is the Problem, Piglet, to which I am asking Pooh to give his mind."

Pooh sat on the floor which had once been a wall, and gazed up at the ceiling which had once been another wall, with a front door in it which had once been a front door, and tried to give his mind to it.

"Could you fly up to the letter-box with Piglet on your back?" he asked.

"No," said Piglet quickly. "He couldn't."

Owl explained about the Necessary Dorsal Muscles. He had explained this to Pooh and Christopher Robin once before, and had been waiting ever since for a chance to do it again, because it is a thing which you can easily explain twice before anybody knows what you are talking about.

"Because you see, Owl, if we could get Piglet into the letter-box, he might squeeze through the place where the letters come, and climb down the tree and run for help."

Piglet said hurriedly that he had been getting bigger lately, and couldn't *possibly*, much as he would like to, and Owl said that he had had his letter-box made bigger lately in case he got bigger letters, so perhaps Piglet *might*, and Piglet said, "But you said the necessary you-know-whats *wouldn't*," and Owl said, "No, they *won't*, so it's no good thinking about it," and Piglet said, "Then we'd better think of something else," and began to at once.

"I've thought up another verse and refrain," said Piglet.
"Oh. All right, how do they go?"
"Like this . . ."

There's not much you can see
When you can't see things at all—
They're too far above your head.
They're for someone
Who is Someone,
Not for someone who is like you . . .

How can I become Bigger?
How can I become Tall?
When will I stop feeling weak, and
When will I stop feeling small?

"That's all very nice, Piglet. I mean as a song. But it's not getting you anywhere, you know."
"What do you mean?" asked Piglet.
"I mean, that attitude won't do you any good. If you keep repeating that sort of thought, you'll

just convince yourself that you're powerless. Isn't that why you feel so afraid?"

"Well," said Piglet, "when you're only a Very Small Animal—"

"If I might make a suggestion . . ."

"Yes?"

"First of all, the fears that push *you* about are not legitimate, appropriate responses to What Is, such as warnings of danger ahead. Instead, they're the constricting fantasies of What *If*: 'What if I should meet a Heffalump, or fall on my face, or make an utter fool of myself?' Isn't that true?"

"Yes . . . I suppose so."

"I would suggest that the next time a What If starts badgering you, look it straight in the eyes and ask it, '*All right, what's the very worst that could happen?*' And when it answers, ask yourself, '*What could I do about it?*' You'll find there always will be something. Then you'll see that you can have power in any situation. And when you realize that, the fears will go away."

"They will?"

"Especially when you realize where the power comes from. In one way or another, we're *all* Very Small Animals, and that's all we need to be. So why worry about it? All we have to do is live in harmony with the Way, for the benefit of the world, and let its power work through us. Let *it* do the work."

"Oh," said Piglet.

"For example, I'm not writing this book. That would be Struggle and Difficulty. Instead, I'm letting the book write itself, through me. That's Fun and Excitement. It flows along, and I follow as best I can. Day by day, wherever I go, things come to me and I include them in these pages. To paraphrase my favorite Haiku writer, Matsuo Bashō, 'Every bend in the road brings me new ideas; every dawn gives me fresh feelings.' Writing with the Way is a journey. And so is everything else. Who knows where the Way will take us tomorrow, and what it will have us doing?"

"I never thought of it like that," said Piglet.

"So you see, as long as we follow the Way, we won't be intimidated by fears—neither fear of failure nor fear of success."

"Fear of *success*? Is there such a thing?"

"There certainly is, and it has a great deal of power over a great many people. Chuang-tse wrote some things about it. Here's one of them":

Yao was seeing the sights at Hua when the border guardian recognized him and approached, saying

"Ah, Master! Blessings on the Master! May he live long!"

"Hush!" said Yao.

"May the Master have much wealth!"

"Hush!"

"May he have many sons!"

"Hush!"

"How is this?" asked the border guardian. "Long life, much wealth, and many sons are what everyone wishes for. Why do you not want them?"

"Many sons," said Yao, "mean many worries. Much wealth means much trouble. Long life means long suffering of abuse. These interfere with the cultivation of Virtue. That is why I do not want them."

"Before," the border guardian replied, "I thought you were a Master. Now I see you are only a Superior Man. Heaven, in sending you sons, is sure to have fashioned occupations for them. If you had many sons, and they had their occupations, what would you have to worry about? If you had much wealth and shared it with others, what trouble would you have? As for long life . . .

"The wise man finds his dwelling like a quail, without worries or struggle. He is fed like a fledgling, by the all-providing Way of Heaven. He travels through life like a bird in flight, leaving no trace as he passes. When the empire follows the Way, he shares in the prosperity. When it loses the Way, he retires and cultivates his Virtue. After many years of contented living, he leaves this world and rides the white clouds. No evil will have reached him. He is free from misfortune. What abuse has he suffered?" With this the border guardian turned and walked away.

Yao followed him. "Wait!" he called. "I would like to ask—"

"Oh, go away!" replied the border guardian.

"That story," I said, "illustrates what the Taoists mean by 'Treat gain and loss as the same.' They mean don't be Intimidated. Don't make a Big Deal of anything—just accept things as they come to you. The Universe knows what it's doing. So don't develop a big ego, and don't be afraid."

"Oh," said Piglet. "I see."

"Going out?" I asked.

"Yes," he said. "I'm going to work on my song."

"Owl," said Pooh, "I have thought of something."

"Astute and Helpful Bear," said Owl.

Pooh looked proud at being called a stout and helpful bear, and said modestly that he just happened to think of it. You tied a piece of string to Piglet, and you flew up to the letter-box with the other end in your beak, and you pushed it through the wire and brought it down to the floor, and you and Pooh pulled hard at this end, and Piglet went slowly up at the other end. And there you were.

Yes, there you were. Unless, as Owl pointed out, the string should happen to break . . .

"It won't break," whispered Pooh comfortingly, "because you're a Small Animal, and I'll stand underneath, and if you save us all, it will be a Very Grand Thing to talk about afterwards, and perhaps I'll make up a Song, and people will say 'It was so grand what Piglet did that a Respectful Pooh Song was made about it.' "

Piglet felt much better after this, and when everything was ready, and he found himself slowly going up to the ceiling, he was so proud that he would have called out "Look at *me!*" if he hadn't been afraid that Pooh and Owl would let go of their end of the string and look at him.

"Up we go!" said Pooh cheerfully.

"The ascent is proceeding as expected," said Owl helpfully. Soon it was over. Piglet opened the letter-box and climbed in.

Then, having untied himself, he began to squeeze into the slit, through which in the old days when front doors *were* front doors, many an unexpected letter that WOL had written to himself had come slipping.

He squeezed and he squoze, and then with one last sqooze he was out.

And Victory was theirs. And so was Help and Rescue. Which just goes to show—

"Here I am again," said Piglet.
"So you are. Another verse, is it?"
"Yes. And refrain."
"Refrain, too? Good—let's hear them."

There's not much you can say
When others, Big and Tall,
With their great muscular
Strength and all,
Find they can't do what you can do,
And you stand there, not feeling small.

What if I had been bigger, and
What if I had been tall?
Think what I would have missed out on—
Not too small, after all.

"Much better," I said. "A great improvement. Well done, Piglet. All around."

"Thank you," said Piglet, looking a good deal Pinker than before.

"Ah—here are Eeyore and Owl. Come on, everybody—we're off to celebrate Piglet's Brave Escape! I've a table reserved at the Six Pine Trees. We'll have to stop at Kanga's for the others, and then—"

"Will there be cake?" asked Pooh hopefully.

"Yes, I believe that's on the menu. Honey cake."

"With—with pink icing?"

"Yes. And there'll be Haycorn Loaf, and—oh, why *talk* about it? Come on, Piglet, don't lag behind."

"Yes, come along," said Pooh. "And bring the rest of your song."

"I'm coming . . ."

Why should I have been bigger, then?
Why should I have been tall?
Why should I have been different, then,
After all?

THE DAY OF PIGLET

They had got a rope and were pulling Owl's chairs
and pictures and things out of his old house so as
to be ready to put them into his new one. Kanga
was down below tying the things on, and calling
out to Owl, "You won't want this dirty old dish-
cloth any more, will you, and what about this carpet, it's all in holes," and Owl was calling back
indignantly, "Of course I do! It's just a question
of arranging the furniture properly, and it isn't a
dish-cloth, it's my shawl." Every now and then
Roo fell in and came back on the rope with the
next article, which flustered Kanga a little because
she never knew where to look for him. So she
got cross with Owl and said that his house was a
Disgrace, all damp and dirty, and it was quite
time it did tumble down. Look at that horrid
bunch of toadstools growing out of the floor there!
So Owl looked down, a little surprised because he

didn't know about this, and then gave a short sar-
castic laugh, and explained that that was his
sponge, and that if people didn't know a perfectly
ordinary bath-sponge when they saw it, things
were coming to a pretty pass. *"Well!"* said Kanga,
and Roo fell in quickly, crying, "I *must* see Owl's
sponge! Oh, there it is! Oh, Owl! Owl, it isn't a
sponge, it's a spudge! Do you know what a spudge
is, Owl? It's when your sponge gets all——" and
Kanga said, "Roo, dear!" very quickly, because
that's *not* the way to talk to anybody who can spell
TUESDAY.

Just what is it that Owl's house reminds us of?
It seems so familiar, somehow. Let's go over it as
though it were still standing—perhaps that will
help us make the association. Let's see . . . It looks
down on all around it, as if tempting the forces of
the natural world to knock it over. It has been
sliding into disrepair for quite some time, as its
proprietor has neglected its necessary maintenance
for other things. It . . . Oh, yes—*that's* what it
reminds us of: our civilization. Will *it* fall down,
too? We wish we could say, "I wonder what will
happen to it." But we can't say that, because we
know.

It's intriguing, and rather Eerie sometimes,

how history tends to repeat itself. The Us First, War Lord Confucianists criticized by Lao-tse and other ancient Taoists seem to have put on new clothes and come back again to take charge. Reading the *Tao Te Ching*'s descriptions of the society of its time, one gets the strangest feeling that they were written the day before yesterday. So once again, Taoism—for all its great age—seems very up-to-the-minute. And once again, perhaps it has something to offer.

Because, we believe, it is not exactly Progress for our nation to have moved from the enlightened era of President John F. Kennedy (was it the Merest Accident that he quoted occasionally from the *Tao Te Ching*?) into an era of scandal-ridden administrations run by Special Interests' Candidates seemingly bent on dismantling our democracy and destroying the nation's land, air, and water in the process, while wrapping themselves in the starry flag of Patriotism. For years now, intelligent, concerned activists have been Out, and self-centered, ignoramus conservatives have been In. And that is not what we'd call the Way of a Healthy Society.

Why these people are called Conservatives is beyond our understanding, as they never seem to *conserve* anything. They don't conserve natural resources. They use them up as quickly as possible. They don't conserve morality and the family, despite much self-righteous boasting to the contrary—boasting that falls rather flat when it comes from those who amass money through commercial enterprises that make a mockery of moral values and put impoverished families, widows, and orphans into the street. They certainly don't conserve *money*. Not taxpayer money, anyway. It would appear that about the only things they do conserve are the very things the human race ought to have discarded long ago: narrow-mindedness, intolerance, coldheartedness, bigotry, *machismo*, and greed.

The Conservatives (being very religious people, they say) believe that "God helps those who help themselves." And so they help themselves to everything they can get their hands on. But don't expect them to help anyone else. And don't expect them to help the earth.

In recent years, for example, our nation's "conservative" leaders have started a war to take Kuwait's oil supply back from Iraq, waging that war by authorizing the bombing of offshore oil rigs (contributing to the largest oil spill in history), goading the opposing forces into igniting 30 percent of Kuwait's oil wells, killing a quarter of a million people (many of them civilians far from any military targets) in what is now known as the most environmentally destructive war in the history of warfare. The bill: 60 billion dollars. They have trashed the energy conservation measures of their predecessors, all but eliminated funding for solar energy research and development, handed the wealthy nuclear power industry a taxpayer-funded boost, pressed for oil drilling in wildlife refuges and coastal waters, refused to authorize the long-overdue and increasingly costly cleanup of toxic waste sites, and so on, and on and on. With wasteful, destructive "leaders" such as these, who needs enemies?

Unfortunately for those of us who would prefer to go on to bigger and better things—such as the advancement of humanity and the assurance of its survival—the great majority of political leaders now in power seem to care for nobody but themselves. And, as in days of old, that means War.

At present, billions of American tax dollars are being spent each year on preparations for war, weapons of war, industries of war—running the

nation into unpayable debt while across the country untaxed gang lords cruise about in limousines,
drug pushers and psychopaths prey on neglected
children, homeless grandmothers push their
worldly possessions before them through the
streets in shopping carts, and citizens of all ages
contract Pistol Fever, shooting themselves and
each other with handguns at the rate of sixty-four
deaths per day—killing more Americans in two-
and-one-half years than did the sixteen-year Viet-
nam War (and wounding approximately one hundred thousand others yearly).

The huge-like-us Soviet Union went Broke
feeding the military, and we're following close behind. Meanwhile, little Germany and little Japan,
who comparatively speaking spend next to nothing
on military matters, are beating us in practically
every area of endeavor. What do we receive in
return for the trillions of dollars that we've handed
to the Armed Forces over the past thirty years?
Let's see. . . . Well, we've been provided with
warplanes that don't fly; armored tanks that don't
steer; weapons that don't fire. . . . No, those don't
count. That's what we're told, anyway. Oh, there
must be something. . . . Ah, yes—half a million
tons of hazardous waste per year. The military is

the nation's largest producer of it. What good *that* will do us is rather hard to say, however. And toxic waste isn't exactly the sort of thing we can return to the store for a refund.

Of course, that waste is sooner or later bound to leak out. Fourteen thousand four hundred military sites are now officially recognized as toxin-contaminated—the cleanup of which is expected to cost taxpayers over two hundred billion dollars—making the U.S. military the country's leading Earth Abuser. The military now directly manages about twenty-five million acres of public land and "borrows" around eight million more from agencies such as the U.S. Forest Service—which allows one hundred sixty-three military training activities in fifty-seven national forests, involving three million acres. How respectfully do the Armed Forces treat the land they manage? Well . . .

The U.S. Army Corps of Engineers describes Basin F of Colorado's Rocky Mountain Arsenal as "the most contaminated square mile on earth." Thousands of animals and birds have died by drinking or landing in its water. Nevada's "Bravo 20" range is a sixty-four-square-mile moonscape after fifty years of battering. In 1983–1984, water from Stillwater National Wildlife Refuge overflowed into the area and mixed with the chemicals in its bomb craters, then receded back into the refuge—killing seven million fish and thousands of birds. Twenty-three million artillery, tank, and mortar shells have blasted the forests and meadows of Indiana's ninety-square-mile Jefferson Proving Ground. Approximately one-and-one-half million of these rounds have not yet exploded. Many are below the surface, nearly impossible to locate. An expert has stated that to decontaminate the once-unspoiled area, it would be necessary to remove thirty feet of ground using armored bulldozers—thirty feet down for ninety square miles.

"When the empire follows the Way," wrote Lao-tse, "horses haul wagons of fertilizer through the fields. When the empire loses the Way, horses haul war chariots beyond the city walls." And:

> *I have three treasures,*
> *Which I guard and keep.*
> *The first is compassion.*
> *The second is economy.*
> *The third is humility.*
> *From compassion comes courage.*
> *From economy comes the means*
> *   to be generous.*
> *From humility comes responsible*
> *   leadership.*

Today, men have discarded compassion
In order to be bold.
They have abandoned economy
In order to be big spenders.
They have rejected humility
In order to be first.
This is the road to death.

The Taoist ideal is to rule by "filling stomachs and building bones"—to take care of society from the bottom up. Today's leaders in government, business, and industry "take care of society" by giving more and more money and power to those at the top. And the Buck Stops There. As Lao-tse described the situation:

The court is filled with splendor.
The fields are full of weeds.
The granaries are empty.
The powerful wear costly clothing,
Carry sharp swords,
Pamper themselves with lavish food
    and drink,
And possess riches in extravagance.
These are not princes and lords.
They are robber barons.

Pooh had found Piglet, and they were walking back to the Hundred Acre Wood together.

"Piglet," said Pooh a little shyly, after they had walked for some time without saying anything.

"Yes, Pooh?"

"Do you remember when I said that a Respectful Pooh Song might be written about You Know What?"

"Did you, Pooh?" said Piglet, getting a little pink round the nose. "Oh, yes, I believe you did."

"It's been written, Piglet."

The pink went slowly up Piglet's nose to his ears, and settled there.

"Has it, Pooh?" he asked huskily. "About—about——That Time When?——Do you mean really written?"

"Yes, Piglet."

The tips of Piglet's ears glowed suddenly, and he tried to say something; but even after he had husked once or twice, nothing came out. So Pooh went on.

"There are seven verses in it."

"Seven?" said Piglet as carelessly as he could.

"*Ahem*," said a squeaky voice.

"Oh—Piglet."

"Yes. Have you seen Pooh?"

"Not lately. But now that you're here, I'd like to ask you something: How are you being treated these days?"

"Amazingly well," he replied. "Yesterday, two people asked me for my autograph."

"Ah. Then the news has been getting about."

"Yes—and it's been rather exciting, really."

"And how has *Eeyore* been behaving toward you?"

"I wouldn't know," said Piglet, "as I haven't seen him for some time."

"Well—*that's* an improvement. Pardon me. Poor old Eeyore. I ought to be more tolerant."

"He does have a good deal to worry him,"

said Piglet. "It's a troublesome sort of thing, being an Eeyore."

"We all have things to worry about," I said. "You've tended to worry quite a bit, yourself. But you took action despite your worries. That's the difference between you and Eeyore. *One* of the differences, anyway."

"Just the same," said Piglet. "We oughtn't be too harsh on Eeyore. I'm sure he'd appreciate a little Kindness."

"I must be running along," he added. "I need to find Pooh. Good-bye."

Well.

"You don't often get *seven* verses in a Hum, do you, Pooh?"

"Never," said Pooh. "I don't suppose it's *ever* been heard of before."

"Do the Others know yet?" asked Piglet, stopping for a moment to pick up a stick and throw it away.

"No," said Pooh. "And I wondered which you would like best. For me to hum it now, or to wait till we find the others, and then hum it to all of you."

Piglet thought for a little.

"I think what I'd like best, Pooh, is I'd like you to hum it to me *now*—and—and *then* to hum it to all of us. Because then Everybody would hear it, but I could say 'Oh, yes, Pooh's told me,' and pretend not to be listening."

If we seem a bit Pigletish at this point, a bit Wary of wholeheartedly endorsing blind optimism in a business-as-usual future, perhaps it's because we live in a nation that with 5 percent of the world's population consumes 25 percent of the world's energy, emits 25 percent of the world's greenhouse-effect-producing gases, yet does not regulate carbon dioxide emissions. While Germany and Japan have for years been reaping the economic benefits of major investments in energy conservation— making Germany's plan the model for the entire European Economic Community—our nation, at ever-increasing cost to the economy, has almost totally ignored such matters and has spent its money on you-know-what.

Yes, we have our doubts about how much love

this country truly has for the earth. Doesn't such love begin at home? Yet even a quick glance inside the typical American house and garage would reveal a startling number of anti-earth chemical weapons with which to keep the forces of the natural world at bay. And outside . . . Americans dump sixty-seven million pounds of pesticide onto the nation's lawns each year—more than farmers use to grow the nation's pesticide-laden food. Some of the thirty-four chemicals used in these Lawn Wonders have not been government tested since the 1940s. Ninety percent of the other seventy thousand chemicals used daily in the United States have never been directly tested for toxic effect.

If we appear a bit Hesitant to embrace the belief that we can go on behaving in such an irresponsible manner without paying the inevitable price, perhaps it's because we live on a planet on which fifteen to twenty species of life are driven to extinction every day, over seventy-five acres of trees are cut every minute, one-third of the land area has become desert, and life-threatening droughts and floods are becoming increasingly common year after year. In Southern Chile, under the emissions-caused hole in the earth's ozone layer—which is four times larger than the United States, and growing—dark glasses, hats, and full clothing in midsummer are becoming commonplace as carcinogenic ultraviolet-B radiation jumps to an estimated 1,000 percent of the pre-hole amount on peak days. In the same area rabbits, sheep, and fish blinded by apparently ultraviolet-ray-induced cataracts are being found in

ever-larger numbers. In Antarctic waters, the
ozone hole has caused an estimated twenty-five-
percent reduction of phytoplankton—the basis of
all life in the ocean.

And so when we hear Big Talk about growing
environmental awareness and about man's ability
to solve any problem, we can't help but wonder
Who's Kidding Whom.

Then we go to the natural world, watch, and
listen. And it tells us that a Great Storm is rising,
and that before long things will become very Interesting—very Interesting, indeed.

We would like to pass along something that
we've learned directly from the earth, as well as
from Taoists, Tibetan Buddhists, Native Americans,
the writings of the prophet Isaiah, and others: A new
way of life is coming—one so unlike today's that it
would be difficult, if not impossible, to describe in
today's terms. We might call it The Day of Piglet.

Before it begins its approach, we'd say to
those people who haven't had the inclination or
the time to become acquainted with the natural
world: Never mind—you'll be getting acquainted
with it, anyway. Because over the next few years,
the natural world will be coming to *you* (although
not necessarily in the way you'd like it to). Perhaps

you might benefit by beginning your acquaintance with it now. Just a suggestion.

Here lies a tree which Owl (a bird)
  Was fond of when it stood on end,
  And Owl was talking to a friend
Called Me (in case you hadn't heard)
When something Oo occurred.

For lo! the wind was blusterous
  And flattened out his favourite tree;
  And things looked bad for he and us—
I've never known them wuss.

Then Piglet (PIGLET) thought a thing:
  "Courage!" he said. "There's always hope.
  I want a thinnish piece of rope.
Or, if there isn't any bring
A thickish piece of string."

"Hello, Eeyore," I said. "We were just talking of you."

"Behind my back, of course," replied Eeyore. "Skullduggery and whatnot. One can't know what to expect these days. Even from one's friends. If one *has* friends."

"Stop that nonsense, Eeyore. Of course you have friends. Piglet, for one. He was just now telling me to be Kinder to you, in light of your difficulties."

"He said *that*? Little Piglet said *that*? That fine, upstanding young pig said *that*?"

Well.

But to conclude what we were saying . . . Whether many people realize it yet or not, man, the Inferior Animal, has by now proved himself incapable of keeping his own species—and others—alive for very much longer. So the earth has begun its own plan to set things right. True to its generous, gentle, and loving spirit, it has been giving us one warning after another of what it will be doing—doing, we wish to emphasize, for the sake of human survival. The sensitive are receiving the messages. But one day when they least expect it, the *in*sensitive will suddenly find themselves Out in the Cold, rather like the mammoths found every now and then up north encased in ice, with once-fresh vegetation in their mouths and an "I say—who just shut off the heat?" look in their eyes. As we understand it, the major cause of What's Coming is the present-day denuding of our planet—the massive overcutting of its forests.

American citizens are spending one billion tax dollars a year to subsidize the U.S. Forest Service's Giant Giveaway of old-growth public forests to the logging industry and Japan, causing countless native animals and birds to lose their homes. By now, ninety-six percent of the nation's original forest has been removed. Meanwhile, the government of China is permanently employing forty-five million people in reforestation, making tree planting a compulsory subject in schools, and decreeing that every Chinese citizen over the age of eleven must plant from three to five trees a year. (The smaller children are being taught to plant grasses and flowers.) Maybe these people Know something.

"Back again, eh? Did you find Pooh?"

"No," replied Piglet. "I don't know *where* he is. Hello, Eeyore."

"Ah," said Eeyore. "Friend Piglet. Not like some around here."

"Eeyore," said I, "have you seen Pooh?"

"Yes. I have. He's a rather short, roundish Bear—pleasant personality, but not particularly intelligent, if you know what I—"

"Yes, yes. But do you know where he *is*?"

"No."

"Oh, here he comes, Piglet—with Rabbit."

"Pooh," asked Piglet, "did you remember to help Owl remove that—"

"Of course," said Pooh. "I have a phonographic memory, you know."

"You mean," said Rabbit, "a *photo*graphic memory."

"No," insisted Pooh. "*Phono*graphic. It goes around and around. Sometimes it gets stuck. That's why I remember things so well."

"So you took care of it," said Piglet.

"Took care of what?" asked Pooh.

Yes. But let's continue, shall we? We'd like to suggest a thing or two that might help us through the previously mentioned Approaching Transition.

As we hope we've shown by now, Taoism is not an Unbending Path. After all, Taoism follows Tao—and Tao does not operate in a rigid, unyielding manner. As Lao-tse emphatically stated in the first line of the *Tao Te Ching*, "The Way that can be followed [literally: "The Way that can be the Way"] is *not* a changeless way" (a line usually translated as "The Way that can be told is not the Eternal Way"). Traditionally, Taoism is considered the Way of the Dragon—the dragon being the Chinese symbol of transformation. Considering the Bad Press that dragons have received in this part of the world, perhaps a better image would be that of the Butterfly. Whatever the symbol used, Taoism is a Way of Transformation—a way through which something is changed into something else.

It is fitting that for centuries Taoists have been associated with magic, as Taoism is, on one level or another, a form of magic—a very *practical* form, perhaps, but magic all the same. Here we will briefly describe two secrets of that magic—two principles of Taoist transformation that may prove Useful in the coming years. The first is Turn the Negative into Positive. The second is Attract Positive with Positive. Unlike some other Taoist secrets, there is little danger of these principles falling into the Wrong Hands; because in the wrong hands, they won't work. We might add that they work best for Piglets.

Turn the Negative into Positive is a principle well known in the Taoist martial arts. Using it for self-defense, you turn your attacker's power to your benefit by deflecting it back at him. In effect, he swings his fist and hits himself in the face. And after a while, if he has any intelligence at all, he stops and leaves you alone.

Transforming negative into positive, you work with whatever comes your way. If others throw bricks at you, build a house. If they throw tomatoes, start a vegetable stand. You can often change a situation simply by changing your attitude toward it. For example, a Traffic Jam can be turned into an Opportunity to Think, or Converse, or Read, or Write a Letter. When we give up our images of self-importance and our ideas of what *should* be, we can help things become what they need to be.

In a similar way, negative personality traits can be transformed. Self-centered stubbornness can be changed into a selfless devotion to an altruistic cause. A desire to control others can be turned into a desire to take control of one's own life and improve oneself—and help others do the same. A tendency to become lost in details can be transformed into the ability to connect things carefully together, step by step, to reach a goal. Indecisiveness can be developed into versatility, and a balanced point of view. And so on.

> *So to the letter-box he rose,*
> *While Pooh and Owl said "Oh!"*
> *and "Hum!"*
> *And where the letters always come*
> *(Called "LETTERS ONLY") Piglet sqoze*
> *His head and then his toes.*

> *O gallant Piglet (PIGLET)! Ho!*
> *Did Piglet tremble? Did he blinch?*
> *No, no, he struggled inch by inch*
> *Through LETTERS ONLY, as I know*
> *Because I saw him go.*

The following is one of our favorite examples
of someone who turned the negative into positive.

In January 1838, the immensely popular English writer Charles Dickens was in Yorkshire
under an assumed name, carrying out a personal
investigation of some boarding schools he had
been hearing about since his childhood. It didn't
take him long to discover that the rumors he'd
heard of brutalized unwanted children had been
understatements. In an accusation against schoolmaster William Shaw dictated by a pupil who had
gone blind in his care, Dickens read that "Supper
consisted of warm milk and water and bread. . . .
Five boys generally slept in a bed. . . . On Sunday
they had pot skimmings for tea, in which there
was vermin. . . . There were eighteen boys there
beside himself, of whom two were totally
blind. . . . In November, he was quite blind and
was then sent to a private room where there were
nine other boys [gone] blind. . . ."

On a dreary afternoon, with snow covering the
ground, Dickens wandered through a Yorkshire
cemetery, counting the graves of children who had
been turned over to the cheap district "schools."
One gravestone read: "Here lie the remains of
George Ashton Taylor . . . who died suddenly at

Mr. William Shaw's Academy. . . ." Upon reading the inscription, Dickens conceived a character for his next novel—a poor wreck of a boy named Smike, who would be tormented by a vicious schoolmaster and die. That next novel would be *Nicholas Nickleby*, and it would be written to focus attention on the schools Dickens had seen, and—to use his own word for it—to *destroy* them. Within a few years after publication of *Nicholas Nickleby*, public outrage had caused all of the Yorkshire prisons-as-schools to be permanently closed.

Throughout his literary career, Charles Dickens drew upon his dark childhood experiences— shy, impressionable young Charles forced to labor ten hours a day in a rat-infested warehouse, his father imprisoned for debt—to shine light into the shadows of complacent Victorian society, exposing the effects of socially tolerated cruelty and neglect through his "entertainments." For he worked as an entertainer rather than reformer. He was wary of social reformers, as they tended to turn people away from the causes they so seriously championed, thereby unwittingly weakening their own efforts.

Charles Dickens preferred instead to charm his London-centered audience with stories of lightness and humor, creating an atmosphere of warm security in which readers *knew* that all problems would be resolved and goodness would triumph in the end . . . And then into this comforting world-on-paper, he would introduce those whom polite society would prefer to ignore—the poor, the forgotten, the abused, the stepped-on. And a society that had long looked the other way began to give attention to its unfortunates.

Coming from a dreary childhood in a shaky family, in which the father was not much of a father nor the mother much of a mother, Charles Dickens almost single-handedly created through his influence the solid, supportive Victorian family and its most colorful expression, the family Christmas celebration we know today. He was also largely responsible for the modern (but now endangered) belief that childhood is an extremely important time of life, one that deserves honor and protection.

During the Christmas season, Dickens—a skilled amateur conjurer—would entertain the children of his family and friends, transforming a bran box into a guinea pig, pulling a plum pudding from an empty pan, sending coins flying through the air, as the children shrieked with laughter.

Charles Dickens was a conjurer of sorts throughout his life, magically transforming the world around him into something better than it had been before. In doing so he gave hope to the hopeless, especially the lost, defenseless children about whom no one of public influence and power had previously seemed to care. And to them, at least, he was far more than an entertainer. When he died, his grave at Westminster Abbey was visited by thousands of admirers. Among the many floral tributes left at the gravesite were, as his son described them, "small rough bouquets of flowers tied up with pieces of rag."

He ran and ran, and then he stood
  And shouted, "Help for Owl, a bird
  And Pooh, a bear!" until he heard
The others coming through the wood
As quickly as they could.

"Help-help and Rescue!" Piglet cried
  And showed the others where to go.
  Sing ho! for Piglet (PIGLET) ho
And soon the door was opened wide
And we were both outside!

Sing ho! for Piglet, ho!
Ho!

"Hello, Kanga. What have you there?"

"The postman was at my house a short while ago," she said, "and he left this letter for Piglet by mistake."

"He did? That's strange—he's usually here by now. But no delivery, as yet."

"There may not be for some time," she said. "Tigger's run off with the mail sack."

"Oh, he has, has he? By now, my catalogues and bills may be lost in the Hundred Acre Wood. Well, I hope he's made a good job of it."

"I'll seek it out," said Rabbit, taking command of the situation at once. "And Owl—we'll need you to search from the air. Come with me, Eeyore. And Pooh, and Piglet—"

"Piglet stays here," I said. "This letter looks Important."

While Piglet's opening his letter, let's take a look at the principle of Attract Positive with Positive. It may be easier to recognize its power if we first recall its opposite, the Eeyore Effect. If we tell children often enough that they are Clumsy, Ugly, Stupid, or Incapable, they will in time become just that. At some level, the mind accepts and retains repeated statements and beliefs as the truth, even though they may be far from it. The sensitivity of Piglets makes them particularly vulnerable to this sort of influence. But it also makes them more than ordinarily capable of positive transformation. Which is why Taoism emphasizes the cultivation of Piglet qualities, as well as the importance of positive attitudes and values.

"I don't know what to make of this," said Piglet. "Why don't you have a look?"

"This *is* impressive, Piglet. It's from Sandhurst University—Pemberton Q. Throckmorton, M.A., Ph.D., etc."

" 'Piglet, Esq. My Dear Sir: The Board of Regents of Sandhurst University wish me to inform you of their desire to grant you an honorary degree of Brave Animal (B.A.). We should be most pleased if you could be present at the awards ceremony, which shall be held on . . .'

"Piglet, that's wonderful! An honorary degree from Sandhurst! Well, well. Now you'll have something to hang on your wall. I didn't know they did that sort of thing."

Let's see—where were we? Oh, yes.

As a basic example of attracting positive with positive, Taoist medicine believes that the secrets of health are found in health. So Taoists study the principles of health and long life—mental and emotional, as well as physical—and work in cooperation with them. In contrast, industrial technology-drugs-and-surgery medicine believes that the secrets of health are found in illness, so it studies disease and death. Consequently, the typical Western hospital is not so much a place for the rehabilitation of the ill and injured as it is a battleground on which medical soldiers, armed with the latest, most expensive weapons, wage relentless war against Unhealth.

A similarly negative, warlike approach can be seen at work in the world of business, especially in its Western half. A successful individual appears to succeed because he is Aggressive—he chases after things and gets them. Chances are his positive attitude attracts those things to him and creates opportunities for success to happen. But chances are onlookers see Aggression succeeding, rather than Attitude. So that's what they imitate. And, since aggression attracts more aggression, the want-to-be-successful turn business into Busyness, creating an atmosphere of increasing combative-ness and negativity in which relatively few are likely to be successful—and even fewer are likely to be happy.

"Know the masculine, but keep to the feminine. . . . Return to the infant state." "Children, who play life, discern its true law and relations more clearly than men, who . . . think that they are wiser by experience, that is, by failure." "Great man retains child's mind." The great man, we would say, plays like a child and attracts like a woman. His play may be serious and his attraction seem masculine on its surface, but they are childlike and feminine nevertheless.

And that brings us to someone we consider the greatest Piglet of all time, who changed his life and the lives of millions by applying the tremendous power available to those who attract positive with positive. We will introduce him with these words by Chuang-tse:

> If a great master ruled the empire, he would stimulate the minds of the people by working in harmony with them, so they carried out his teachings unconsciously and without rebelling. Under his influence they would reform their manners, the evil and violence within them would be extinguished,

and they would move forward as individuals acting for the common good, as if they did so on their own initiative.

Could such a leader be compared to even the greatest names in recorded history? He would come from a time before any of them existed. His only desire would be to bring other minds to rest in the Virtue of those long-forgotten days.

As a small boy, Mohandas Karamchand Gandhi was frail and shy. "My books and my lessons were my sole companions," he later wrote. "To be at school at the stroke of the hour and to run back home as soon as the school closed—that was my daily habit. I literally ran back, because I could not bear to talk to anybody." For years he would not go out at night. As a young man, he went to England to study law. "Even when I paid a social call," he wrote, "the presence of half a dozen or more people would strike me dumb."

But Mohandas Gandhi was a Learner. He learned from his studies. He learned from being the perpetual Piglet. And from his parents he learned, in time, some of the most important lessons of his life.

From his father he learned the importance of

bravery, generosity, and unwavering adherence to the principles of morality and truth. From his mother he learned the importance of gentleness, modesty, and consideration, as well as the flexible strength that enables one to overcome through yielding. From both he learned that if one wants positive results, one must be positive, and that goodness persistently applied will always triumph over evil, even though it may seem to take a good deal of time doing so.

Eventually, through applying what he learned to the advancement of one Underdog Cause after another, Gandhi became known as quite a fighter, winning battles that many older, more experienced campaigners told him could not be won. He not only won them; he did so by, as the Chinese saying puts it, "fighting without fighting."

Encountering massive, statutory discrimination against Indians in South Africa, Gandhi began a campaign of nonviolent resistance. In jail for his respectfully uncompliant behavior, he read and was inspired by Henry David Thoreau's essay "Civil Disobedience." But words like "resistance" and "disobedience" bothered him. Wanting a more positive term, he and a cousin came up with *Satyagraha*, or Truth Power.

Gandhi said that Truth Power would overcome opponents by changing them with respectful,
patient persistence—transforming them, not anni-
hilating them. Again and again, he was told it
would not work. And again and again, despite
overwhelming odds, it did.

In South Africa, Truth Power brought about the
Indian Relief Bill. In India, it achieved the granting
of democratic reforms; united long-separated political
territories, parties, and factions; stopped civil war;
revived home industries; freed the nation from Brit-
ish rule; and freed the "untouchables" from the ages-
old caste system that had persecuted and imprisoned
them. It earned Gandhi—who held no government
office, but led India just the same—a popular respect
so high that he could exact political concessions by
fasting. And it earned for him, despite his strong
distaste for it, the title of *Mahatma*, Great Soul.
Gandhi insisted that he was no god—the success of
Satyagraha in his life, he said, showed that anyone
could achieve similar results.

Wherever Gandhi went, he transformed situations and lives. As one friend and biographer
wrote, "He . . . changed human beings by regarding them not as what they thought they were but
as though they were what they wished to be, and
as though the good in them was all of them."

Many descriptions have been written of M.K. Gandhi and his Truth Power movement. But our favorite has never, we believe, been quoted. It was written by Lao-tse centuries before Mohandas Gandhi's birth, in chapter after chapter of the *Tao Te Ching*:

Nothing in the world is more yielding and gentle than water. Yet it has no equal for conquering the resistant and tough. The flexible can overcome the unbending; the soft can overcome the hard.

• • •

Why is the sea the king of ten thousand streams? Because it lies beneath them. Therefore, if the great man would rule the people, he must put himself below them. If he would lead them, he must put himself behind. Then they will neither feel oppressed by his weight nor threatened by his prominence. The world will delight in pushing him forward, and will never tire of him.

• • •

A good commander does not rush ahead. A good fighter does not show anger. A good conquerer does not antagonize. A good employer does not act superior. This is called "the Virtue of not striving," "making use of the abilities of men," and "matching heaven"—the extreme limit of the ancients.

• • •

I am good to those who are good. I am good to those who are not good. And so all attain good-

*ness. I am sincere to the sincere. I am sincere to
the insincere. And so all attain sincerity.*

•   •   •

*Fine weapons are instruments of evil. All crea-
tures hate them. Therefore, followers of the Way
do not use them. . . . To rejoice over victory by
violence is to rejoice over slaughter. He who re-
joices over slaughter cannot unite all within the
empire. . . . The wise ruler sees a military triumph as a funeral.*

•   •   •

*The violent die violently—that is the foundation
of my teaching.*

•   •   •

*Yield and prevail. Bend and be straightened.
Empty and be filled. . . . The great man embraces
the One, and becomes its model to the empire. Not
showing off, he shines. Not asserting himself, he
becomes known. Not taking credit, he is ac-
claimed. Not boasting, he endures. He does not
strive against others, so others do not contend
with him. The ancients said, "Yield and prevail."
Is that a worthless saying? Put it into practice,
and all things will come to you.*

Many say that Lao-tse's advice to those who
would rule (or manage their own lives) is pleas-
ant-sounding but impractical—that in real life it
couldn't work. Yet in real life it did work. One
might even say it worked miracles. But Mohandas

K. Gandhi wouldn't have put it that way, any more than Lao-tse would have. He knew all too well what such "miracles" consist of: the patient, persistent application of the laws of spiritual transformation, especially that of Attract Positive with Positive.

"We're back!" said Pooh.

"*Mission Accomplished,*" announced Rabbit.

"And we've quite a surprise for Piglet," said Owl.

"So you have. All this mail—is for *Piglet?*"

"So it is," said Pooh.

"From Admirers," Owl added.

"For *me?*" said Piglet, in a throaty sort of squeak. "I—I don't know what to say."

"Then don't say anything," remarked Eeyore gloomily.

"*Eeyore,*" I cautioned. "Remember what Piglet said about—"

"I only meant," explained Eeyore, brightening considerably, "that in cases of this sort, there is nothing one *can* say."

"That's better."

"Especially if one is Exceptionally Modest and Self-Effacing. Like Piglet."

"Much better."

"Or like myself."
"Hmmmmm."

As Taoists have long observed and remarked
on, something taken to its extreme turns into its
opposite: Extreme *Yang* (masculine) becomes *Yin*
(feminine), and so on. The present age of man—
an extreme if there ever was one—might well be
called the Age of the Warrior. Man against man,
man against the earth . . . So, according to the
Taoist principle, the coming age will be an Age of
the Healer, or something of the sort. But first will
come what could be called a Great Purification.

As our planet takes action to cast out its man-
made poisons and heal its man-caused wounds,
many human inhabitants will no doubt give way to
fear. Many will cling to seemingly powerful we're-
God's-chosen-people religions, hoping that by so
doing they will be saved from the wrath of a
Vengeful God (not recognizing that the approaching "vengeance" will in reality be man's own
actions coming back at him—and not recognizing
that the Infinite Universal Power is far more than
the narrow-minded gatekeeper of an exclusive
Spiritual Country Club). Many will find themselves in the wrong place at the wrong time, be-

cause they did not pay enough attention to what the natural world was telling them. And many will curse the world, and believe that they have been cursed by it.

But in reality we are the most fortunate generation since recorded human history began. For when the necessary cleansing is over, we will witness a magical transformation of the world around us by the forces of the earth. And we will see for ourselves what the ancient Taoists meant by the Age of Perfect Virtue.

When the remains of today's anti-earth civilization have been cleared away, we will find ourselves in the state of paradise that existed before the Great Separation occurred. Man's lesson will have been learned—permanently, without the slightest doubt. The wise leadership and light-handed government described by Lao-tse and practiced by Mohandas Gandhi will be universal. And the Day of Piglet will be here.

FAREWELL

We have decided to conclude this Taoist Exposition, or Expotition, or whatever-it-is, with three quotations from Here and There. The first is a Buddhist saying, the second is a selection from the writings of Sir Arthur Conan Doyle, and the third is our abbreviated retelling of a story by Hans Christian Andersen. Just trying to be democratic, you know.

"You do like to borrow things, don't you?" said Piglet.

"Yes," added Eeyore. "And he never puts them back."

Anyway, first we have the Buddhist saying:

In the world of truth, there is no East, no West. Where then is the North, the South? Illusion makes the world close in. Enlightenment opens it on every side.

Next, Sherlock Holmes, in "The Naval Treaty":

"There is nothing in which deduction is so necessary as in religion," said he, leaning with his back against the shutters. "It can be built up as an exact science by the reasoner. Our highest assurance of the goodness of Providence seems to me to rest in the flowers. All other things, our powers, our desires, our food, are all really necessary for our existence in the first instance. But this rose is an extra. Its smell and its colour are an embellishment of life, not a condition of it. It is only goodness which gives extras, and so I say again that we have much to hope from the flowers."

And finally, our shortened version of "The Nightingale":

The emperor of China loved to listen to the singing of the nightingale, which brought him great contentment. One day he was presented with a mechanical bird covered with jewels and gold. To the emperor's amazement, it sang the nightingale's song with perfect clockwork precision, whenever he wanted it to. It quickly became the sensation of the empire—from peasant children to court officials, everyone (or almost everyone) admired the wonderful bird, which sang perfectly, over and over. Ignored and forgotten, the real bird flew away.

But after some time, the clockwork bird broke down. Without its song to soothe him, the emperor became ill. His condition grew worse, until he was nearly at the point of death. Just then, a nightingale alighted outside the window, and began to sing. His will to live restored, the emperor recovered.

And now, since this *is* his book, Piglet's going to give us all a song.

"Are you ready, Piglet?"

"Yes, I (hep) *think* so (hep!)" said Piglet, hiccuping nervously. "It goes like this . . ."

Let's find a Way
Today
That can take us to tomorrow—
Follow that Way,
A Way like flowing water.

Let's leave
Behind
The things that do not matter,
And turn
Our lives
To a more important chapter.

Let's take the time,
Let's try to find
What real life has to offer.
And maybe then
We'll find again
What we had long forgotten.
Like a friend,
True 'til the end,
It will help us onward.

The sun is high,
The road is wide,
And it starts where we are standing.
No one knows
How far it goes,
For the road is never-ending.

It goes
Away,
Beyond what we have thought of;
It flows
Away,
Away like flowing water.

All American Detail

1500 S. Babcock Street
Melbourne, FL. 32901
(407) 727-0319

life time warranty

NAME		PHONE	DATE
Tom		779-9475	4-4-94

STREET		WORK PHONE	

CITY, STATE AND ZIP CODE		VEHICLE	
		'88 Honda Prelude	

T Window tint w/s/s 300-450			85.00
SH #279			
		Sub-Total	
		Tax	5.90
		Total	90.90

	SOLD BY	RECEIVED BY	Ninety one

"Perfect!" I said. "I knew you could do it."

"Have we reached the end?" asked Piglet.

"Yes," I replied. "I suppose so."

"It *seems* to be the end," said Pooh.

"It does. And yet—"

"Yes, Piglet?"

"For me, it also seems like a beginning."